The tragedy is that this book is necessary. We live in a dark and sinful world where atrocities beyond imagination or comprehension occur. How to minister to those who have been so violently assaulted is a pressing and sobering question. The title of this work *The Gospel and Sexual Abuse* points to the only ultimate answer to that pressing question. The gospel of Christ is the answer to every sin and issue of life. Nye effectively demonstrates how to bring the gospel to bear on this devastating situation. The illustrations, examples, analogies, and rubrics for counselling are helpful, but Nye makes clear that the Bible is the touchstone for addressing this tragedy of life. Those who are called upon to minister to those who are so hurting will find this little book to be a useful guide.

Michael Barrett, PhD
Senior Research Professor/Biblical Studies
Puritan Reformed Theological Seminary

The brilliance of the gospel is that it enables God's people to practically walk in Christ's love with those cruelly mistreated by others. While not glossing over the pain of sin, Jesus calls the church to care for – with His grace and truth – those who have been shattered by sin. Although not a simple subject to tackle, sexual abuse is not beyond the hope and ethics of the gospel. Sadly, in their attempt to help, too often churches have naively done more damage than good, because of a hesitancy to seek guidance in the complexities of dealing with the perpetrators of and caring for victims of sexual abuse. To that end, Todd Nye's timely book, *The Gospel and Sexual Abuse,* addresses with Gospel grace and Biblical truth the painful real-world issues involved in the care of sexual abuse survivors. The great benefit of this book is three-fold: First, it is bathed in the Gospel grace of Jesus, which sweetens the sourest of experiences. Second, it is saturated with God's Word without rejecting God's wisdom also revealed through common grace. Third, it reflects decades of the pastoral experience of a man of God, Todd Nye. I highly recommend this work as a resource to those who care for others in and through the church.

David Saxton, ThM
Pastor, Cambridge Bible Church
Cambridge, OH

Writing a book to bring healing to victims of abuse and to address forgiveness to the perpetrators of it is as commendable and necessary as it is intimidating. Todd Nye has presented, not an easy way, but a sure way to healing and forgiveness. The conscientious and specific examination of biblical teaching sets out violated duties and unmerited rights before divine perfection as the foundation for healing and reconciliation. Todd shows that God has made a way through the trauma of abuse. Todd's alert and affirmative writing tone, a welcome human and compassionate resonance throughout the book, adds more than just what such a book needs to be—it expresses, but also breathes, the hope that the God who ably made the universe readily restores the individual.

Dan Hurst
Trinity College

In *The Gospel and Sexual Abuse*, Pastor Todd Nye has harnessed his experiences counseling people impacted by sexual sin and has set forth the sufficiency of the gospel as it is embraced by those who suffer. Drawing on examples from his ministry and the experiences of others, he displays the adequacy of the gospel of Jesus Christ as the only healing balm for sufferers wounded deep in their souls, as well as for perpetrators crushed by the weight of their sins. Here, counselors will find a guide map to assist others lost in their confusing dark valley of pain. Here victims will find a pathway to real peace. This work sets forth the power of the gospel to destroy Satan's work in one dark corner of human suffering, but its relevance is not limited to this single arena of sin. Readers will be encouraged to "apply the ethic of the Gospel" to other vistas of their lives where they encounter brokenness, sin and sorrow. In the end they will find the cross of Christ to be a place of personal help and healing.

Steve Brennecke, JD
CEO BMM Foundation
2nd Vice President, Baptist Mid-Missions

The Gospel and Sexual Abuse

*A Healing Balm for Bruised Bodies,
Battered Minds, & Broken Hearts*

T. SAMUEL NYE

 Press

The Gospel and Sexual Abuse
A Healing Balm for Bruised Bodies, Battered Minds, & Broken Hearts

Copyright © 2023 by T. Samuel Nye

Published by G3 Press
4979 GA-5
Douglasville, GA 30135
www.G3Min.org

All rights reserved. No part of this publication may be reproduced, stored in a retrieval system, or transmitted in any form by any means, electronic, mechanical, photocopy, recording, or otherwise, without prior permission of the publisher, except as provided for by USA copyright law.

Printed in the United States of America by Graphic Response, Atlanta, GA.

ISBN: 978-1-959908-15-9

Contents

Introduction 1

Chapter 1 – Preliminary Considerations 7

Chapter 2 – The Mandate for Full DISCLOSURE 17

Chapter 3 – The Demand for JUSTICE 29

Chapter 4 – The Command for CONFESSION 45

Chapter 5 – The Glory of FORGIVENESS 71

Chapter 6 – The Critical Need for CONTAINMENT 127

Chapter 7 – The Call for CLOSURE 149

Conclusion 164

Introduction

Within six months of my first pastoral position, I was immersed in a baptism of fire for which I was utterly unprepared. I met a man canvassing the neighborhood of an old mill town. I was introducing myself and the ministry to the community and telling them of our desire to serve the residents as best we could. After initial visits and getting to know him, he confessed Christ and, from all objective scriptural evidence, was gloriously converted. He was a middle-aged, long-haul truck driver whose face and overall deportment bore the marks of a man who had lived a hard life, notorious for drinking and carousing. He had been married five times. The woman to whom he was married at that time I met him was very different. He was her first husband. She was raised in the strict atmosphere of the Church of Christ (old-line Pentecostal) and was riddled with guilt that her marriage was an act of adultery. She handed me a copy of the Constitution of her church and told me, "You are going to have to unteach me what I have been taught my whole life." The leadership of her church told her, after they were informed of her marriage to a man married four times before, that she had committed adultery and the only way to make it right with God was to divorce him. Among other scriptural points of counsel, I told her two wrongs don't make a right.

Within the same first year of getting to know the family, the live-in boyfriend of his daughter brutally murdered the man's two-and-a-half-year-old grandson. I remember well the foreboding atmosphere of the courtroom in which he was arraigned, charged, and then found guilty by a jury of his peers. He was sentenced to life in prison without parole. It was a baptism in an array of emotionally charged fires. I was totally out of my depth.

Then the bomb hit. The same man, the truck driver in his fifth marriage who made a profession of faith, was arrested for fondling his granddaughter, the young daughter of his own son. The son, a professing Christian who did not want to subject his daughter to the horrors of a fully drawn-out lawsuit, elected that his dad undergo extensive counseling by a professionally licensed counselor. This was a provision made by the state in which he resided. He was not criminally charged and did not spend a day behind bars. I accompanied him to the counseling sessions and learned some tremendous lessons. It forced me to diligently research many of the biblical, pastoral, filial, legal, clinical, psychological, and emotional aspects involved in cases of sexual abuse. Over the next twenty-seven years in ministry, I was asked to be the mediating counselor in three other cases involving differing degrees of sexual abuse. The whole sad affair of sexual abuse raises a thousand questions—questions which must be faced head on and demand thoughtful, sensitive, and truthful

INTRODUCTION

answers that encompass every aspect of such brutal sins against other human beings.

How do you apply the teaching of the Christian gospel to the sad and appalling cases of sexual abuse? How do you counsel both the victims of abuse and those guilty of heinous acts of abuse against another human being? How should every church and parachurch organization establish policy, undergirded by good theology and the clear statements of Scripture, so that they posture themselves in a Christ-honoring way in the face of every alleged or substantiated accusation of sexual abuse? How can we possibly apply a healing balm to the bodies, minds, and hearts of people bruised, battered, and broken by the scandal of an offense rising to the level of sexual abuse?

Lying just east of the Jordan River and slightly northeast of the Dead Sea is the mountainous region of Gilead. Gilead is famous for spices and myrrh. The balm from Gilead, which grew on a little shrub, was a sticky, honey-like resin reputed in the ancient world for its medicinal powers. Most likely, it was a moderate sedative, expectorant, or antiseptic applied as a healing ointment meant to relieve patients experiencing pain. Because of the rich supply of balm in Gilead, there were many physicians located in that region. As a result, the expression "balm in Gilead" was taken up by the prophet Jeremiah (627–586 BC) and used figuratively to speak of something that had spiritual healing powers. As part of his third message to southern Judah he foretold—because of their wickedness, gross spiritual obstinacy, and impenitence—their inevitable doom at the hands of the Babylonians. Their case was incurable! At that critical juncture in the nation's history, he inquired if there were any spiritual physicians who could skillfully apply the balm of Gilead to mollify their spiritual wounds. The cast of professional prophet and priest counselors were so totally inept that it made the case of the nation hopeless. As a result, Jeremiah expressed a nearly inconsolable grief that there was no one who could deftly heal their debased condition:

> They heal the brokenness of the daughter of My people superficially . . . For the brokenness of the daughter of my people I am broken . . . Is there no balm in Gilead? Is there no physician there? Why then has not the health of the daughter of my people been restored? . . . Go up to Gilead and obtain balm . . . In vain have you multiplied remedies; There is no healing for you (Jer 8:11, 21-22; 46:11).

There is a clear modern parallel between this nearly hopeless period in Israel's ancient history and our own time. Our daughters (and many sons, too) are broken by sexual assault. Further, it is sad to say and hard to admit that counselors who might rise with healing wisdom are few and far between. Even sincere efforts to offer healing help are often superficial at best and, at worst, offer ill-conceived remedies that compound the horror. We may justly ask, as did Jeremiah, why then has not the health of the daughters and sons of my people been restored?

MRSA (*Methicillin-resistant Staphylococcus aureus*), known as a "super bug," is a skin infection that can become visually offensive and unimaginably grotesque in the extreme. In worst-

INTRODUCTION

case scenarios, it becomes a deep, invasive infection that spreads to other internal organs. If it appears so ugly on the surface, what must it look like when waging an all-out assault on the internal well-being of the physical body? What makes MRSA so difficult to treat is that the bacteria is resistant to an entire class of penicillin-like antibiotics called beta-lactams. It is no overstatement to suggest that a sexual assault against another person is to their entire spiritual being what MRSA is to the physical being. Further, the treatments traditionally offered to victims of sexual abuse can prove to be totally ineffective because the wounds inflicted by sexual abuse are often resistant to an entire strain of counseling, especially those ill-conceived by unqualified practitioners. The way it presents on the exterior is appalling in the extreme, but the outside merely masks an even more sinister and vicious attack against the person's emotional, psychological, and spiritual well-being. No one in their right mind would ever suggest treating a gaping flesh wound eaten away by MRSA with a little dab of Neosporin covered with a pink colored band-aid. No more should we advocate treating victims of sexual abuse with a quick-fix, one-hour session that hardly detects the surface effects, let alone the soul-threatening disease devouring their entire spiritual being. To do so would be like a physician applying sulfuric acid to the open lacerations caused by MRSA.

The answer to the question of how to respond to cases of sexual abuse is that we must begin with the genius of Scripture and be informed by Scripture at every step. More specifically, since sins of every kind rip gaping wounds in the hearts of people and massacre healthy relationships beyond recognition, we must apply the healing balm of the gospel. The genius of the gospel and the application of its ethic alone has the power to deal with volcanic ruptures of this magnitude. The gospel is the only lasting hope! The Bible is sufficient to outline a course of action to heal the bodies, minds, and hearts of people who have been bruised, battered, and broken by sexual abuse. Let's start this journey with some preliminary considerations that will demonstrate the sufficiency of Scripture to address the issue of sexual abuse adequately and accurately. From that starting point, we can more specifically apply the all-healing gospel balm to this wound.

CHAPTER 1

Preliminary Considerations

*"All Scripture is inspired by God and profitable
... for correction."* (2 Tim 3:16)

Scripture is not silent regarding sexual assault. The first explicit reference forbidding sexual assault is located within the moral structure of the Mosaic law prescribed by God for the nation of Israel.

> But if in the field the man finds the girl who is engaged, and the man forces her and lies with her, then only the man who lies with her shall die. But you shall do nothing to the girl; there is no sin in the girl worthy of death, for just as a man rises against his neighbor and murders him, so is this case (Deut 22:25–26).

So grave is the sin of sexual assault that under the righteous code of God's unbending theocratic law, it was viewed as a crime necessitating capital punishment. Furthermore, the victim is regarded as not bearing any responsibility whatsoever for an assault which was forcible and against her will. It was obviously an egregious sin against the very dignity of her person. Two other passages that record notorious cases of sexual assault give a window into the patently disgusting nature of the sin and the devastating effects that result from it. Genesis records the rape of Dinah at the hands of Shechem (Gen 34:1–2), and the book of Judges records the gang rape of a Levite concubine at the hands of vile men. It then describes in brutal detail the unspeakably ghoulish reaction to cut the victim into twelve pieces and disperse her body parts throughout the twelve tribes. The Ephraimite dismembered her body to graphically illustrate the depravity to which the entire nation sunk (Judg 19:22–26).

The passage, however, that gives us the clearest picture into the awful sin of sexual molestation is the incestuous rape of King David's daughter, Tamar, at the hands of her half-brother, Amnon. In the narrative account of his appalling crime, Amnon is depicted as utterly detestable, and the author takes pains to describe the victimization of Tamar through her eyes and from her perspective. After faking an illness as a pretense to seduce her, 2 Samuel 13:11–17 records the despicable actions of Amnon—

> When she brought them to him to eat, he took hold of her and said to her, "Come, lie with me, my sister." But she answered him, "No, my brother, do not violate me, for such a thing is not done in Israel; do not do this disgraceful thing! As for me, where could I get rid of my reproach? And as for you, you will be like one of the fools in Israel. Now

therefore, please speak to the king, for he will not withhold me from you." However, he would not listen to her; since he was stronger than she, he violated her and lay with her. Then Amnon hated her with a very great hatred; for the hatred with which he hated her was greater than the love with which he had loved her. And Amnon said to her, "Get up, go away!" But she said to him, "No, because this wrong in sending me away is greater than the other that you have done to me!" Yet he would not listen to her. Then he called his young man who attended him and said, "Now throw this woman out of my presence, and lock the door behind her."

In the record of this rape, the word "violated" means to inflict pain upon a person by force.[1] The horror and profoundly disturbing repercussions of such violently forceful sexual assaults is strikingly described from Tamar's point of view—

> Second Samuel 13 provides an insightful analysis of sexual assault, because it is portrayed through Tamar's eyes. Tragically, her experience includes manipulation, force, violence, negation of her will, emotional trauma, debilitating loss of sense of self, display of grief and mourning, crushing shame, degradation, forced silence, and prolonged social isolation with desolation. Tamar's social and personal boundaries are clearly violated.

---

[1] R. Laird Harris, Gleason L. Archer, and Bruce K. Waltke, *Theological Wordbook of the Old Testament* (Chicago: Moody Press, 1980), 682.

It's clear in verses 12, 14, and 22 that Amnon's actions of assault are violating, shaming, forceful, and humiliating. Violence permeates his words and actions. The words used to describe Amnon's feelings and physical state express sick emotions rather than life-giving ones. According to Phyllis Trible, Amnon reduces Tamar to the state of a "disposable object." After he assaults Tamar, Amnon commands her to leave by telling his servant, "Get this woman out of my sight." Amnon barely speaks of her as a person. She is a thing Amnon wants thrown out. To him, Tamar is trash.[2]

The sexual assault of Tamar, as recorded in 2 Samuel and described so graphically in *Rid of My Disgrace* is no G-rated psychological presentation. The accurate depiction of the sexual assault of Tamar—involving "manipulation, force, violence, negation of her will, emotional trauma, debilitating loss of sense of self, display of grief and mourning, crushing shame, degradation, forced silence, and prolonged social isolation"—provides a clear, yet disturbing window into the things experienced by victims of abuse.

Since the ancient biblical record of sexual abuse does not articulate either a specific legal or psychological definition, a comprehensive and modern definition of sexual assault is essential. While the following definition is specifically related to the abuse of children, the elements of such assaults can be applied more broadly—

---

[2] Justin S. Holcomb and Lindsey A. Holcomb, *Rid of My Disgrace: Hope and Healing for Victims of Sexual Assault* (Wheaton, IL: Crossway, 2011), 20.

PRELIMINARY CONSIDERATIONS

Child sexual abuse is defined as any sexual activity with a child where consent is not or cannot be given. This includes sexual contact that is accomplished by force or threat of force, regardless of the age of the participants, and all sexual contact between an adult and a child, regardless of whether there is deception or the child understands the sexual nature of the activity. Sexual contact between an older child and a younger child also can be abusive if there is a significant disparity in age, development, or size, rendering the younger child incapable of giving informed consent. The sexually abusive acts may include sexual penetration, sexual touching, or noncontact sexual acts such as exposure or voyeurism.[3]

While it is not the purpose of this book to deal with a comprehensive definition of all forms of abuse, an extremely helpful resource can be found in Mez McConnell's riveting book, *The Creaking on the Stairs*. In the chapter entitled, "What Do We Mean By 'Childhood Abuse'?", he uses multiple sources to give a helpful and rather expansive definition of multiple forms of abuse: childhood maltreatment, contact and non-contact forms of sexual abuse, physical abuse, emotional abuse, and neglect.[4]

---

[3] "Adult Manifestations of Childhood Sexual Abuse, Definitions," American College of Obstetricians and Gynecologists, Aug 2011, https://www.acog.org/clinical/clinical-guidance/committee-opinion/articles/2011/08/adult-manifestations-of-childhood-sexual-abuse.

[4] Mez McConnell, *The Creaking on the Stairs: Finding Faith in God Through*

With such accurate legal definitions in place, along with the biblical portrayal of the rape of Tamar, it helps us to view abuse in exactly these terms. Sadly, mounting evidence, ever-increasing statistics, and a non-stop flood of mainstream accounts clearly indicate we have been and continue to live in a culture of abuse. More horrifying than the staggering statistics is that sexual abusers, ironic in the sickest way, are often protected and sheltered. This is aggravated immeasurably and inexplicably by the fact that those who protect such ravenous wolves and venomous snakes are sometimes churches and religious organizations who refuse to report such cases to the proper authorities and who give abusers asylum in their demented shelters. This is not a phenomenon unique to twenty-first-century America. In Ezekiel 34:2–4, the prophet denounced the shepherd-leaders of Israel in one of the most scathing rebukes to be found anywhere in Scripture. The diatribe against them, among other things, included a rebuke that the entirety of their spiritual oversight was effectively abusive.

> Son of man, prophesy against the shepherds of Israel. Prophesy and say to those shepherds . . . "Those who are sickly you have not strengthened, the diseased you have not healed, the broken you have not bound up, the scattered you have not brought back, nor have you sought for the lost; but *with force and with severity you have dominated them.*"

Childhood Abuse (Fearn, Ross-shire: Christian Focus, 2019), 30–37.

PRELIMINARY CONSIDERATIONS

In the face of such undeniable realities, assuming the task of counseling those who have been so abominably abused is one for which very few are qualified. Even when sincere counselors have approached the delicate task of helping a victim of abuse with the best of motives, they may exacerbate the problem. By a course of advice lacking any real understanding of the psychology of the abused, they can exponentially increase the agony of the abused. Some Christian counselors, as a first line course of action, have ignorantly assumed that an appropriate approach to counseling those abused is to inquire whether they were complicit or did anything to provoke the abuser. Cases that involve a teenager that is just barely of legal age with a teenager one year younger might legitimately ask if the sexual interaction was consensual. But to initiate a biblical approach to counseling a victim of sexual abuse by inquiring whether the abused created the temptation and needs to confess and repent of such temptation is ignorant at best. At worst, it becomes another act of abuse against a person already reeling from atrocious acts against the very dignity of their person.

One indisputable fact, supported by years of analyzing the pathology of those sexually abused, is that the abused might, in the most perplexing way and depending on the severity of the abuse, feel that the perpetrator was showering on them some special attention. This is particularly relevant with the youngest victims of abuse, where the abuse most often comes from someone within or very close to their family. Betrayed in the most awful way by someone they have every reason to trust sets off an array of the most conflicting and confusing responses.

They may, on an inexplicable level that testifies to just how grave the sin against them is, derive a misguided sense of security and even emotional pleasure.

> It is not uncommon for some victims to be physically aroused at some point during the assault. If victims experience any emotional gratification or physical pleasure during the assault, they might feel a sense of guilt or shame that further reinforces the already distorted negative self-image.[5]

As shocking and immensely troubling as this is, it figures into just how egregiously the perpetrator has sinned against them and violated the sacred identity of a person made in the image of God. Not only have they been physically and sexually abused, but they have been spiritually, emotionally, and psychologically traumatized in the extreme. The evidence of the degree of the trauma is seen in the horrifically abnormal ways their minds can potentially respond. By a twisted and perverted violation of their person, the abuser shapes a view of the abused person's self-image that is mangled and distorted beyond recognition.

In other studies, children who have been molested by their fathers, as part of the indescribable pain of being sinned against by the person who is supposed to love and protect them the most, have convoluted feelings of the most bizarre kind. Monumental feelings of guilt arise because in one breath they

---

[5] Justin S. Holcomb and Lindsey A. Holcomb, *Rid of My Disgrace: Hope and Healing for Victims of Sexual Assault* (Wheaton, IL: Crossway, 2011), 71.

wish they could hate their father, but in the next are incapable of doing so. They undoubtedly wish they could hate him with all their heart but mixed in with the putrid feelings of disgust toward their father are those aspects of love for him where he, at times, showed them some level of care. It is classified by clinical psychologists as "traumatized bonding," in which a child experiences alternating periods of love mixed with episodes of abuse.

> Clinical psychotherapy continues to struggle with examining why some severely abused children have trouble disconnecting from their abuser and forgetting them. Some children, as difficult as it is to believe, continue to desire the nurturing and accepting love of an abusive parent, even long after they have been removed from the abusive home environment. Some individuals who have endured long-term abuse often find themselves harboring conflicting emotions. There are times when the abused individual may hate the abuser one minute and the next minute make statements or do things that makes the relationship appear better than it actually is. . . . Most individuals who are the victims of abuse desire love and affection, sometimes only the love and affection of the abuser. It's almost as if the person desires the love and affection of the abuser so much that they will do anything to achieve it.[6]

---

[6] Tamara Hill, "9 Signs of Traumatic Bonding: "Bonded to the Abuser," *Psych Central*, September 9, 2015, https://blogs.psychcentral.com/caregivers/2015/09/9-signs-of-traumatic-

These facts speak to the unspeakable and disturbingly profound effects that sexual abuse has on the abused. None but the abused can ever possibly understand just how life-altering are the effects. Even the efforts to describe the impact on the abused in this volume are only approximate attempts at real accuracy. Consequently, few are equipped to counsel victims of sexual abuse through the hell on earth that this brings about in their life. Furthermore, to offer "Christian" counseling from anything less than a healthy familiarity with the related literature and an informed understanding of the psychological, medical, clinical, legal, biblical, and pastoral issues in play is reckless beyond description. Doing so (even if counseling with the purest of motives) may exponentially cause more damage. A good beginning recommendation when counseling any victim of sexual abuse within the church or Christian organization is to immediately insist on outside intervention and to ensure the prime pastoral counsel come from a man with experience in this area and who is a well-seasoned minister of the gospel. Mature and well-trained women also play a valuable and indispensable role in such counsel; even taking the lead when circumstances require it (Titus 2:3–4).

A balancing consideration to the need for "expert" counseling in all the related fields is necessary at this point. To be qualified as a pastor-counselor addressing the broad spectrum of issues affecting human behavior does not require the pastor to hold a PhD in counseling, let alone advanced training in the

---

bonding-bonded-to-the-abuser/.

other sciences mentioned above (i.e., psychological, medical, clinical, and legal). A thorough acquaintance and growing mastery of scriptural truth and wisdom, as well as a distinctively biblical approach to counseling, should be sufficient to equip the pastor-counselor to guide the abused and those guilty of abuse. Furthermore, there are multiple resources to assist pastors when they feel they are out of their depths and need specialized help and counsel.[7] Consequently, given the few resources mentioned in the footnote, ignorance of and negligence about the input of these other disciplines is rather inexcusable.

Applying then the ethic of the gospel of the Lord Jesus Christ to cases of sexual abuse, any thorough discussion must encompass at least the following six considerations: disclosure, justice, confession, forgiveness, containment, and closure.

---

[7] Christian Counseling & Educational Foundation, https://www.ccef.org/ (CCEF); Association of Certified Biblical Counselors, https://biblicalcounseling.com/ (ACBC); International Association of Biblical Counselors, https://www.iabc.net/ (IABC).

CHAPTER 2

The Mandate for Full DISCLOSURE: Uncovering the Wound

". . . all things become visible when they are exposed by the light." (Eph 5:13)

Similar to Jeremiah's inconsolable grief that no prophet or priest could apply a healing balm to the injured daughters of his people, he also lamented their complete unwillingness to expose such hideous spiritual wounds; "they have not exposed your iniquity so as to restore you from captivity" (Lam 2:14).

In the initial stages of bringing cases of sexual abuse to light, the facts of the case are typically made known to only a limited number of people. Later, when allegations are confirmed by evidence and based upon the specific facts of the case, the circle of people notified must be broadened appropriately—in some cases, broadened extensively. The application of the ethic of the gospel of Christ in such cases, in the most general sense, endorses, encourages, and mandates full disclosure of the sin.

More specifically, the Scripture mandates a precise methodology for full disclosure.

Implications When Sin is Not Confronted and Exposed

In the most preferred way of disclosure, the perpetrator comes under enough conviction of sin by the Holy Spirit or feels the searing pangs of conscience so deeply that they come forward of their own initiative. More likely, because of the immense level of loathsome shame and the twisted character of the perpetrator, the abused is often compelled to report the sinful crime and bring out into the full light of day the sins committed against them. This needed disclosure is exactly the ethic Jesus commanded in cases of sin. In the first and preferred case, the perpetrator initiates the exposure of sin.

> Therefore if you are presenting your offering at the altar, and there remember that your brother has something against you, leave your offering there before the altar and go; first be reconciled to your brother, and then come and present your offering (Matt 5:23–24).

In this scenario, our Lord makes it emphatic that the failure to pursue a course of reconciliation with someone against whom you have sinned, regardless of how much time has transpired since the time of the initial sin, absolutely prevents the person from true worship. It nullifies any possibility of ongoing communion with God unhindered by sin. This is the most profound implication when sin is not addressed and brought to light—it severs any claim to a functionally healthy relationship with the Lord. This not only applies to what we regard to be grave sins but is true of all unconfessed sin when we refuse to deal with it. The statement, "if you are presenting your offering at the altar," clearly refers to a person trying to engage God in an act of worship. The words that follow, "leave your offering there before the altar and go; first be reconciled to your brother, and then come and present your offering," clearly indicate fellowship with God is terminated until the sin is disclosed by a full, truthful, and unequivocal admission of the guilt. It is an admission, in harmony with the ethic of the gospel, that seeks forgiveness of the sin.

If the perpetrator does not initiate full disclosure, then the person on the receiving end of the sin must come forward. Disclosing the sin, as delicate and challenging as this can be, is initiated by the victim who has obviously been wounded immeasurably. Yet, even in this case, the ethic of the gospel must be applied. Disclosing and exposing the sin of the perpetrator must be motivated out of loyalty to the gospel ethic and out of Christ-like love for the person guilty of the sin. In this case, the offended party is admonished—

> If your brother sins, go and show him his fault in private; if he listens to you, you have won your brother. But if he does not listen to you, take one or two more with you, so that BY THE MOUTH OF TWO OR THREE WITNESSES EVERY FACT MAY BE CONFIRMED. If he refuses to

listen to them, tell it to the church; and if he refuses to listen even to the church, let him be to you as a Gentile and a tax collector (Matt 18:15–17).[1]

More generally, while this is clearly a divine mandate when sins are committed by one Christian against another in the household of God, the ethic embodied in the general principal can rightly be applied in contexts other than the local church. Furthermore, extending the principle beyond cases of sexual molestation, Jesus, in the most unambiguous terms, describes the implications when sin is not dealt with—regardless of who commits the sin and how severe:

> Make friends quickly with your opponent at law while you are with him on the way, so that your opponent may not hand you over to the judge, and the judge to the officer, and you be thrown into prison. Truly I say to you, you will not come out of there until you have paid up the last cent (Matt 5:25–26).

---

[1] In circumstances when a younger person is violated by an older person, especially when the abuser is over 18 and therefore legally considered an adult pedophile, the abused should *not* initiate contact with the perpetrator. Because of obvious reasons as well as legal concerns and the protection of the child, the first step of the process outlined in Matthew 5:15–17 should be tailored to the situation and, within our legal system and the judicious wisdom of the church, the abused should not interact with the perpetrator alone and should ask for intervention immediately and from a qualified outside source.

THE MANDATE FOR FULL DISCLOSURE

As a passage strongly emphasizing the urgency of reconciliation, Jesus does not draw these words from the legal systems of his day because he is concerned about Jewish legal jurisprudence. Nor is He primarily concerned about the division that takes place on the horizontal relationship caused by sin. He uses this illustration to warn against the danger of hell fire if you, as a guilty sinner, are not reconciled to God by both admission and confession of your sin. This transcends any specific sexual sin against another person and applies to sin in general. Jesus is so emphatic we implement this divinely inspired process for dealing with sinful offenses that He amplifies the point in two ways.

First, He advises a specific four-stage process for dealing with accusations of sin: 1) confrontation, 2) confirmation of facts, 3) public correction, and 4) the possibility of excommunication in cases where the sinner is impenitent in light of verifiable evidence. *Secondly,* He throws the full weight of His divine authority behind the process: "Truly I say to you, whatever you bind on earth shall have been bound in heaven; and whatever you loose on earth shall have been loosed in heaven" (Matt 18:18). Binding and loosing were the most commonly used terms by Rabbis in Jewish canon-law and were understood to represent the legislative and judicial powers of the Rabbinic office. Jesus's use of the terms was a cultural way of stamping with divine approval the entire process for dealing with sin. The ultimate outcome of exposing the sin of another person is not always certain, but the authority of Christ mandates the exposure because of the grave implications if it is not dealt with at all.

The Tendency to Cover Up

Sadly, clear-cut cases of sexual violations by staff members of local churches, as well as those serving parachurch organizations, have been proven beyond any shadow of a doubt. We have all watched such cases play out in the media. What's more pathetic is when overwhelming evidence is brought out into the full light, we witness people lie and try to cover their sin. Rather than frank admission of guilt and humble confession of sin, we witness men, constrained by Satan and their own corrupt sinfulness, concealing rather than confessing their sin. Proverbs 28:13 applies this beyond cases of sexual abuse and more generally to all sin—"He who conceals his transgressions will not prosper, but he who confesses and forsakes them will find compassion."

Jesus Himself clearly described the dynamic when men attempt to cover their sin and avoid exposure at all costs. This dynamic is in play whenever sinful men shrink and recoil at the full exposure of their sin—

> This is the judgment, that the Light has come into the world, and men loved the darkness rather than the Light, for their deeds were evil. For everyone who does evil hates the Light, and does not come to the Light for fear that his deeds will be exposed (John 3:19–20).

THE MANDATE FOR FULL DISCLOSURE

One of the distinguishing indicators of a genuine experience of salvation is that the saved person, as a part of "coming to the light," does not resist the exposure of his sin.

In fact, because of the convicting operation of the Holy Spirit (John 16:7–8), there is a willingness to allow God to bring his sins into the light. This willingness is seen by the new humility to confess his sin rather than deny it. "But he who practices the truth comes to the Light, so that his deeds may be manifested as having been wrought in God" (John 3:21).

Years ago, a ruptured copper water line forced me to make a repair in my basement late at night. The lighting in the crawl space was terrible, so I used a bright flashlight to illuminate the area where I was working. To support the copper pipe I was attempting to solder, I picked up a short piece of a 2x4 that was lying near me and lodged it under the pipe. When I pulled the piece of wood off the dirt floor, countless roaches, and insects, invaded by the light, scurried to return to the repose of their dark nooks and crannies. Repulsed by the light of exposure, they were in full and furious retreat. It is the same way when the light of God's truthful exposure of sin blinds the eyes of sinful men living comfortably and undisturbed in their pitch-black abode. Like a vile and disease-ridden insect, impenitent sinners will not come to the Light for fear that his deeds will be exposed. It seems that extreme sexual violations against another person (especially the young, innocent, and vulnerable) greatly magnify this tendency to retreat into lies. Rather than honestly confessing their guilt, they retreat and cover up. When any person, church, or parachurch organization does this, it results in the complete removal of trust and credibility.

In short, the ethic of the gospel must be applied to general acts of sin in our world, and it must be specifically applied, in the most informed and deft way, to cases of gross sexual misconduct. Without the full disclosure of sin, the needed process is ignored and the issue between two sinners can never be made right. Thankfully, while we think the full exposure, admission, and confession of our sin will be embarrassing in the extreme and ruinous to our reputations, by the grace of God through the application of the work of Christ such exposure is the only pathway to forgiveness and reconciliation. If you are guilty of such a sinful crime or are the victim of such a sinful crime, the Bible assures you that full disclosure is the only God-sanctioned way to deal with it and the first critical step to forgiveness, healing, and reconciliation. It does not break us to expose, confess, and forgive sin; it makes us!

If you are a victim of abuse, none of us who have not been so abused can ever begin to understand the level of uncertainty that must cloud your thinking as you consider disclosing the facts of your abuse. Further, none of us can come close to appreciating the level of courage it takes to disclose such abuse. What can assure us all, regardless of the trauma that must mark such offenses, is that God's revealed will teaches us that full disclosure is the first vital step toward dealing with sin appropriately and is essential for the healing process to begin.

Far and away, the most monumental example of barefaced exposure of sin is the model of God Himself in providing the only way for the forgiveness of man's sin. When Christ hung and died on the cross as a substitutionary atonement (a vicarious substitution) for the sins of mankind, it was not only an infinite exposure of the awfulness of sin, but of the infinite judgement, mandated by God's justice, which demanded the full penalty for sin. God did not nor could not minimize the magnitude of man's sin. In pouring upon His own Son the just wrath which our sins deserve, His own sterling example is one in which He did not gloss over or cover sin in the least—but fully exposed and dealt with it! As the classic example of full disclosure of sin, God dealt with it by laying all the sins of mankind directly on His Son as the necessary judgment for the sins we commit. Linking the full disclosure of sin with the judgement of God against sin is critical to understanding the ethic of the gospel.

The book of Romans teaches that the future judgement against all those who reject Christ and do not disclose and confess their sins will be a staggering apocalypse (a full disclosure) of God's immeasurably intense judgement:

> But because of your stubbornness and unrepentant heart you are storing up wrath for yourself in the day of wrath and revelation of the righteous judgment of God . . . but to those who are selfishly ambitious and do not obey the truth, but obey unrighteousness, wrath and indignation. There will be tribulation and distress for every soul of man who does evil (Rom 2:5, 8–9).

God's anger against sin, expounded in the most descriptive literary terms in Romans 2, can be defined as an internal emotion under such pressure that it is swelling with an agitated impulse to explode in a breath of violent eruption. Like a heated cauldron fueled by intense flames, it will finally boil over. To those upon whom it spills, it will be an unimaginable cause of immense distress and anguish. No, God does not gloss over sin! It must be fully disclosed, and it must be righteously punished. This is the ethic of the gospel *par excellence*.

The reason there is not one millisecond of judgment to be feared by the Christian is because, on the cross, all of God's fury, God's burning anger, God's holy hostility, and all God's pent-up wrath against sinners was poured out relentlessly and without reserve in infinite measure on Christ. God will never have to fully and finally expose the sin of those who have confessed and repented of their sin, precisely because He exposed the sin and executed the just judgment against it in the person of Christ. This took place when God the Father "made Him who knew no sin to be sin on our behalf, so that we might become the righteousness of God through Him" (2 Cor 5:21). The reason it is impossible for God to ever level against any Christian an infinitely immeasurable showcase of His pure hatred of sin is because that is exactly what He did when the Lamb of God was struck down by His own hand and sacrificed in our place: "For Christ also died for sins once for all, the just for the unjust, so that He might bring us to God" (1 Pet 3:18). God's own example, when dealing with the raw and revolting nature of all of man's worst sins was to expose it. Exposure was necessary for

THE MANDATE FOR FULL DISCLOSURE

healing. "He Himself bore our sins in His body on the cross, so that we might die to sin and live to righteousness; for by His wounds you were healed" (1 Pet 2:24).

Following the pattern of God Himself, the only way to deal with sin and set the healing motion into process is for guilty offenders to realize the implications of not dealing with sin, to refuse to hide from it in denial, and to actively submit to the full disclosure of their sin.

Points of Practical Pastoral Wisdom	
Primary Goal	In the first stage of applying the ethic of the gospel to cases of sexual abuse, the counselor should strongly encourage and emphasize the absolute necessity of full disclosure!
Real Life Example	A woman I once counseled was compelled to expose a serious moral violation committed by her husband. For her, reporting her husband's sin caused an involuntary convulsion of the most painful guttural emotions, but it was an act of love that resulted in critical help for her husband. The husband was simply humiliated. Both the pain and humiliation of exposure can work against this vital first step.

Vital Questions	What do you think the outcome will be if the issue is not fully exposed? What do you think is making full exposure so difficult? Do you recognize in the physical realm (as in the spiritual realm) that the full exposure of an illness or injury is vital to begin the healing process?
Typical Counselee Responses	The thought of full exposure is often accompanied by forms of hiding, crippling embarrassment, abject humiliation, tactics of diversion, and even total self-delusion. The discerning pastor-counselor will recognize these as hindrances to full exposure.
Specific Applications	Applying the need for full exposure of sin is primarily a scriptural exercise. Using the indicatives of gospel truth related to recognizing sin for what it is (regardless of how hideous) is essential. Then the counselor can move to the imperative demand. This allows the debilitating sin to come into the full light of exposure.
Homework	This will vary from case to case, but the imaginative pastor-counselor will quickly envision the kind of homework that will fix the mind of the abused or abuser on the key scriptural concepts needed to transform their thinking and help them fully expose sin. A helpful assignment would require that they read what caused David to hide his sin of adultery, murder, and manipulation and then what the Lord used to bring him to admission and the full exposure of his sin.

CHAPTER 3

The Demand for JUSTICE: Receiving the Appropriate Penalty for Perversion

"God will bring into judgment both the righteous and the wicked, for there will be a time for every activity, a time to judge every deed." (Eccl 3:17)

The eyes of lady justice are said to be blind. This literary personification of justice is understood to refer to the dispassionate objectivity by which cases are judged, and that gives to our judicial system its moral force. Justitia, the Roman goddess of justice, is depicted in marble statues as blindfolded with a balance in her right hand and a sword in her left. When the blind and objective eyes that judge allegations of sexual abuse are opened by the unmistakable verdict of clear guilt, never is it more important to hold in one hand the scales of justice and to hold in the other hand the sword that we must swing swiftly and fiercely.

Since cases of sexual abuse are judged in both civil courts of law and ecclesiastical courts of law (the church), there arises a potential dilemma: is there an inherent conflict between the two courts? May one court evaluate allegations from a completely different basis than the other, and may one render a sentence of punishment while the other renders a sentence of a completely different kind? As Christians, we must answer this question rightly! We must judge rightly even if the civil courts do not. The only way we can do that is by a thorough understanding of the intended meaning of the scriptural writings and a fearless courage to apply that meaning impartially to all cases of sexual abuse: "I solemnly charge you in the presence of God and of Christ Jesus and of His chosen angels, to maintain these principles without bias, doing nothing in a spirit of partiality" (1 Tim 5:21). Specifically, two questions confront us when guilt is proven beyond any shadow of doubt, and we are forced to discern the proper course of action. 1) Is ecclesiastical justice and civil justice one and the same? 2) Does the church have the moral and spiritual obligation to use the same means of punishment as does the State? These questions must be answered with a yes and a no.

Comparing the Processes Used to Determine Guilt or Innocence

Just as civil courts have a rule of law governing a process for determining guilt or innocence in the face of alleged crimes, so the Scriptures provide both general principles and specific sets of instructions for determining the guilt of any person charged with serious violations of sin. The ethical standards by which the civil courts evaluate allegations are guaranteed to Americans in the Constitution: the rule of law, due process, the right to a fair and unbiased trial by a group of our peers, and a presumption of innocence until proven guilty beyond any reasonable doubt. The ethical standards provided to the church for evaluating charges of sin brought against a Christian have built into them the same assurances as those embodied in the legal jurisprudence of the Constitution. The church must avoid viewing the principles provided to it in cases of serious allegations to be like an "arraignment," where the prosecution looks to indict above all else. We don't, so to speak, have church tribunals. The scriptural principles do, however, advise a way for a "summons," where a person accused of serious sin is brought before biblically-ordained structures of authority to determine if the charges are true. The person charged must have a way to seek redress because of the possibility that another Christian has falsely accused them. The Apostle Paul, when brought to trial before the cruel Roman governor of Judea, Felix, appealed to the justice of Roman law which ensured the same protection:

> I answered them that it is not the custom of the Romans to hand over any man before the accused meets his accusers face to face and has an opportunity to make his defense against the charges (Acts 25:16).

Consequently, while the exact means used to draw a verdict are different between the civil and ecclesiastical courts, they are similar in that they both have a process in place to ensure justice. Matthew 18:15–17, alluded to earlier, outlines the four-step, God-given process for prosecuting a case of alleged, serious sin: 1) confronting the person charged with the specific allegation (summons); 2) confirmation of facts (right to a fair and unbiased trial); 3) public correction (an appropriate level of punishment upon an admission of guilt); and finally 4) excommunication (where the person is refused further affiliation with the church due to impenitence in the face of proven guilt). Several other passages point to these principles, and others spell them out quite specifically. It is quite clear that Scripture teaches there is time to make an accusation and level a charge: "Be on your guard! If your brother sins, rebuke him; and if he repents, forgive him" (Luke 17:3). There is also a necessary caveat to avoid the destruction of another's reputation in the face of a false accusation: "you shall investigate and search out and inquire thoroughly. If it is true and the matter established that this abomination has been done among you" (Deut 13:14). "Do not receive an accusation against an elder except on the basis of two or three witnesses" (1 Tim 5:19).

While there are several other passages of Scripture that teach these values (Lev 6:2–7; 19:17; Num 5:6–7; Prov 25:9–10), the advice given to the Corinthians is very direct. Among the Corinthian Christians, who were wrongfully attempting to litigate cases against other Christians in pagan law courts, Paul gives very clear instructions. He clearly promotes what, under the inspiration of Scripture, is a church sanctioned process for dealing with accusations of sin made by one Christian against another.[1]

> Are you not competent to constitute the smallest law courts? Do you not know that we will judge angels? How much more matters of this life? So if you have law courts dealing with matters of this life, do you appoint them as judges who are of no account in the church? I say this to your shame. Is it so, that there is not among you one wise man who will be able to decide between his brethren (1 Cor 6:2–5).

Comparing the Measures of Punishment When Guilt Is Proven

In cases where the civil or ecclesiastical authorities determine a guilty verdict, both have guidelines determining what constitutes just and reasonable forms of punishment. For either the State or the Church, it is a miscarriage of justice to under-punish with a lenient slap on the hand what should be, if justice be done, a rather severe form of discipline. It is also a miscarriage of justice to inflict punishment excessively and far out of proportion to the crime. We all understand this instinctively. No reasonable parent would ground a fifth-grade boy for a year for stealing a pack of bubble gum. Similarly, two sixteen-year-old teens caught in inappropriate behavior in the back of a church bus on the way to

---

[1] This provision in no way trumps or averts the legal requirements of the law in cases of sexual abuse.

a youth retreat require just reproof and encouragements as to why such behavior puts them in moral jeopardy. But a just response to a pastor embezzling thousands of dollars will require a response far more severe. Over punishing is no trite matter, but in gross cases of heinous sins, miscarriages of justice are especially odious when the punishment is far less than the crime deserves.

A specific example of variations in the severity of the punishment is when the State, compelled because of a guilty verdict, begins to inflict just sentences for cases of gross sexual misconduct. It is a legal fact that the juvenile court system, when doling out just sentences against teenagers who have committed sex crimes, are far more remedial than punitive. The civil legal system seems to recognize that selfish acts and stupid decisions are sometimes attributable to the wild and reckless impulses of severe immaturity. The juvenile courts implement strategies that maximize counsel and re-habilitation. The hope is that such measures, over time and when met by the juvenile's admission and recognition of how criminal and hurtful his actions were, may result in a person no longer being a risk of sexually abusing others. When, however, a person of legal adult age is found guilty of sexual crimes, especially acts of pedophilia, the adult court system is postured to be exclusively punitive—and rightly so!

In civil cases, all violations do not rise to the same level of criminality. Consequently, the laws of each state (though there is a great deal of national consensus in such cases) mandate the extent to which sexual crimes can be punished. Likewise, in cases where the church must execute scriptural and just measures of discipline in the face of indisputable guilt, it must be remembered that all cases do not rise to the same level of severity. Every sexual sin is serious, and every case of sexual misconduct is gravely serious, but the ability to discern the various levels of severity is crucial. Consequently, while every case must be processed biblically and consistently, not every case requires the same extent of discipline. A middle-aged man who misleads a thirty-year-old woman to consensually engage in inappropriate conduct will require the attention of church leadership and will demand actions of discipline in proportion to the sin. A middle-aged man, however, who violates a prepubescent child rises to an altogether different level of gross sinful misconduct and requires a multi-leveled response far different and much more severe than the other.

It is admitted that rating the severity of sexual sins against another person is a tenuous endeavor. For example, gauging such offenses the way we might classify hurricanes, you might consider a fourteen-year-old boy who fondles a twelve-year-old girl, where not even the clothes are removed, to be a Category 1 offense. In other cases, where pedophiles violate children in unspeakable ways, we would classify the offense as a Category 5 to the one-hundredth power. While most people would recognize the importance of differentiating the severity of individual cases of sexual abuse, there is a risk of making a grave mistake. We cannot and must not conclude, because one case of assault is comparatively less extreme than another, that the level of emotional trauma experienced by the victim is less extreme. Years ago, due to chronic back pain, my orthopedic doctor told me that one patient may be bone on bone with a disc protruding so far that it would appear to require immediate surgery. Despite how their condition presents, they may be in little pain or discomfort. Conversely, a person with the slightest evidence of disc deterioration may be in agonizing pain. The greater pain in the patient visually presenting lesser problems is often because the disc is impinging directly on a nerve. The science of dealing with those abused, because the nature of this awful sin against humanity is so precariously speculative, will not allow for a verdict that the lesser severe assault is lesser in terms of psychological trauma.

Threats to Justice in the Current Cultural Climate

Responding to accusations of sexual assault and thus pushing for just and appropriate levels of punishment puts us on a cultural knife's edge. This is true in society at large as well as in the church. The 2017 advent of the #MeToo movement—a movement that arose in protest of sexual harassment and sexual assault—along with the evidence of how widespread sexual abuse in our country is, prompted a just, legitimate, and much-needed reaction. No one could have predicted just how intense the response has been. The prevalence of the problem and the atrocious ways people are bruised in body, battered in mind, and broken in heart completely justifies the blood-curdled screams of any person so violated. The bravery of their willingness to shout this from the mountaintops is to be applauded. The predominance of such crimes and the absurd possibility that they are neither duly processed or left unpunished is an undeniable reality in our culture. The *Chicago Tribune* chronicled an enormous number of cases involving sexual abuse, running from Tarana Burke (a sexual assault survivor), who coined the phrase "Me Too" in 2006, all the way to Roseanne Barr's 2019 controversial testimony on Candace Owens's podcast about the Hollywood culture of sexual manipulation.[2]

While this sad chapter in American history has prompted an understandable level of disgust and outrage, it comes with a potential liability. The entire discussion is fueled with so much raw emotion and uncontrollable volatility that, at times, it threatens the fair and dispassionate assessment when life-altering accusations are made against another person. Every accusation must be taken seriously, and when guilt is proven beyond doubt, lock the door and throw away the key! Mere accusations alone, however, are not sufficient grounds to incriminate a person. Along with demanding justice for victims of abuse, there must be equal demands that such accusations be proven. Everyone knows the capacity of humans, for a great variety of foul reasons, to falsely accuse another person. This fact is exactly why the Constitution of the United States as well as the biblical guidelines for responding to accusations outline a fair and judicious process. Unfortunately, and this is easily demonstrable

---

[2] Christen A. Johnson and KT Hawbaker, "#MeToo: A Timeline of Events," *Chicago Tribune*, March 7, 2019, https://www.chicagotribune.com/lifestyles/ct-me-too-timeline-20171208-htmlstory.html.

by facts; some have made wildly false claims of abuse that stand to ruin beyond repair the reputation of innocent people. In February of 2019, NPR ran a story entitled, "Jussie Smollett 'Took Advantage of the Pain and Anger of Racism.'"[3] He made horrifically false accusations, lying to police about a supposed racist and homophobic attack. Thankfully, and in keeping with upholding the values inherent in the United States Rule of Law, he was tried for such a libelous accusation and indicted on sixteen charges. Still further, it is apparent that others, to advance a political agenda and forcibly push a victim-driven mentality and resentment-ridden ideology, have hijacked the #MeToo movement for villainous and selfish ends. Sadly, such tactics significantly minimize and trivialize the legitimate complaints of persons abused. As a result, credible news outlets have reported on this dangerous tendency:

> "While it's critically important that women who've been assaulted are heard, we cannot forget about the fundamental right to due process that our great country was founded upon," said Andrew Miltenberg, one of the nation's leading due process attorneys. "This is a dangerous time in our nation's history, reminiscent of the days of McCarthyism, where a single accusation is enough to end a career. Even baseless charges can ruin a lifetime of work in some

---

[3] Colin Dwyer, "Jussie Smollett 'Took Advantage of the Pain and Anger of Racism,' Police Say," National Public Radio (NPR), February 21, 2019. https://www.npr.org/2019/02/21/696593870/chicago-police-empire-actor-jessie-smollett-faked-attack.

situations," Miltenberg said. . . . "Historically, false allegations of sexual assault have been a frequent and persistent phenomenon—particularly for Black men."[4]

Between 1958 and 1968, Russian writer and historian, Aleksandr Solzhenitsyn wrote *The Gulag Archipelago*. In short, the title meant to describe the elaborate system of prisons during the Cold War, Iron Curtain period of Soviet Russia. The Gulag, the government agency in charge of the Soviet forced-labor camp system, was a powerful and much feared agency. The Gulag was known to come out of nowhere, accost men, secretly whisk them away, and exile them to places like Siberia without so much as a hint of evidence to justify such radical seizures. Men simply disappeared and their grief-stricken families were made to pick up the pieces of their shattered emotions and go on as if the person never existed. If the legal mechanisms in the courts of the United States and the principles of the gospel ethic are not vigorously applied, the reputations of completely innocent people risk being erased by the mere hint of accusation. It appears we are witnessing the formation of a new bullying Gulag agency—one with great power that accosts innocent people and obliterates their reputation by an assumption of guilt based on scathing accusations made without a hint of justifiable evidence. The accused are virtually made to disappear by a kind of

---

[4] Stacy M. Brown, "Could False Accusations Threaten the #MeToo Movement?" *The Philadephia Tribune*, January 1, 2019, https://www.phillytrib.com/commentary/could-false-accusations-threaten-the-metoo-movement/article_6951dae9-f205-54c6-b95f-8fcde02648b6.html.

accusation-hysteria gone to seed. In fact, the radical hysteria surrounding those pushing false accusation narratives have become so inflamed and pervasive that anyone who refuses to validate such hysteria are, in the justice-perverted mentality of professional slanderers, considered a part of the establishment supposedly enabling the abusers. This is indeed a dangerous time for our country, and it is a dangerous time for churches.

As suggested in the book recommendations in Ben Sasse's New York bestseller, *"Why We Hate Each Other—And How to Heal,* a blind myside-ism, acting with a mob-mentality, is creating a toxic division that threatens the very survival of our Republic. In the words of the Nebraska Senator himself—

> We're living through a revolution that is going to utterly transform the ways we live and work. We're living through an upheaval that will arguably dwarf the disruption our nation experienced a century and a half ago.[5]

Doom and gloom prophecies are not the answer, but this kind of realistic, gut-check analysis is vital if we are to escape the inevitabilities that result when mob-like, myside-ism fills the atmosphere of the cultural conversation and dwarfs the kind of civil, evidenced-based dialogue that can prevent the impending upheaval.

---

[5] Ben Sasse, *Them: Why We Hate Each Other—And How to Heal* (New York: St. Martin's Press, 2018), 2.

Legal Requirements

For the church, then, to alleviate the dangers of wrong responses to allegations of sexual abuse, it must be thoroughly acquainted with the national and state laws legislated to protect its own citizens. It must know even better the legislations of Scripture which are every bit as careful to protect those whose safety should be secure under its protective wings. The church is not a rogue, anarchist organization living by its own rules and flying by the seat of its pants (Rom 13:1–4; 1 Pet 2:13–17). It is governed by Scripture, and those very same Scriptures tell churches to live under the laws of their governing nations—except when those laws directly violate Scripture.

While there are minor variations among the states' laws that comprise the USA, those laws very consistently determine the extent to which churches are required to report cases of sexual abuse. When the church is made aware that a member or attender who is also a citizen of the United States claims they have been sexually abused, the laws make crystal clear how the church is legally obligated to respond. To fail to comply is in direct violation of civil laws and, more importantly, it is to disregard and flagrantly disobey the laws of God: "Submit yourselves for the Lord's sake to every human institution, whether to a king as the one in authority, or to governors as sent by him for the punishment of evildoers and the praise of those who do right. . . . Honor all people, love the brotherhood, fear God, honor the king" (1 Pet 2:13–14, 17). Mediating counselors and pastors have no choice of "discretion" to keep the circle of those who have knowledge of the abuse narrower than the law demands. They must immediately and without delay make all notifications to agencies required by law. To not do so is to clearly sin against God, the victim, and the clear teaching of Scripture.

If the State law allows for a more limited circle of legal notifications when a minor is involved, parents, at their own discretion, may wish to avail themselves of this legal right. When parents do not wish to further expose their minor-aged-children beyond the shame and humiliation they have already experienced; they may elect to have professionally qualified agencies provide the needed counsel rather than pushing the details through every level of the civil courts. The state laws that dictate the mandatory rules for clergy reporting are easily accessible from multiple sources. Know them! Typically, state laws and organizations that exist to educate and protect in cases of abuse, provide helpful information encompassing a broad range of vital issues: "Cross-Reporting Among Responders to Child Abuse and Neglect, Definitions of Child Abuse and Neglect, Immunity for Reporters of Child Abuse and Neglect, Mandatory Reporters of Child Abuse and Neglect, Making and Screening Reports of Child Abuse and Neglect, Penalties for Failure to Report, False Reporting of Child Abuse and Neglect, and Representation of Children in Child Abuse and Neglect Proceedings."[6]

---

[6] The following information is available from The Child Welfare Information Gateway, www.childwelfare.gov.

Church Policies Providing Protection and Accountability

It is vitally important that the church know how to posture herself toward persons who have been guilty of sexual assault against a minor. In cases where an abuser later confesses their sin, truly repents, seeks forgiveness, is granted forgiveness, and willingly submits to the long-term consequences created by their sin (in most cases life-long consequences), the church must have a well thought-out process that takes all the biblically relevant teaching on the subject into account. In some cases, and depending on the extent of the abuse, the perpetrator may totally forfeit the privilege of any further identity and interaction with the church family. In other cases, the leadership must specify what the exact and appropriate measures of discipline must be. They must provide a strict and constantly monitored system of accountability to prevent any further sin of this magnitude. Three considerations compel the church to take such strict measures in cases of sexual abuse against a minor. First and foremost, the protection of children is paramount. Secondly, the integrity of the Christian gospel must be protected against any accusation that the church is neutral or weak in its stance against such blatantly immoral conduct. Thirdly, a church must protect its own reputation against charges of carelessness in this area (these ideas are developed more fully in the chapter titled "The Critical Need for Containment"). The best way to protect the integrity of the gospel and its own reputation is by never providing asylum for a person guilty of abuse. The gospel is protected by a full disclosure and a no-toleration policy. If it fails to do this, it loses its right to be a bastion of spiritual safety for those who seek spiritual guidance and protection within its hallowed sanctuaries.

	Points of Practical Pastoral Wisdom
Primary Goal	In the second stage of applying the ethic of the gospel to cases of sexual abuse, the pastor-counselor must insist on the integrity of biblical justice.
Real Life Examples	Human nature often craves leniency in the face of guilt that requires, if justice is served, full punishment. Humans also thrive on extending leniency where possible. Undue leniency, however, in legal cases that require just punishment, is the cause of much civil upheaval and unnecessary pain. Countless examples of parents letting their children go scot-free in the face of behavior that requires justice is behind the destruction of the character and life of many people.
Vital Questions	What has formed your view of justice? Do you believe that God is always just (fair)? Do think justice can be side-stepped without serious consequences? Does every case of sin need to be pressed to the fullest extent of the law? Do you think you have been treated with justice in your life? The answers to these questions will likely

	establish that the counselee, to one degree or another, believes justice is vital. This is foundational to expounding on the essentials of a biblical approach to justice.
Typical Counselee Responses	Those abused are often tempted by an intense desire for justice with no admixture of grace or mercy. Abusers, when not fully convicted and convinced of the enormity of their sin, will often buck at exacting justice. When the gospel ethic is working by the Word and the Holy Spirit, the abused will desire the forgiveness and deliverance of the abuser from bondage, and the abuser will willingly accept the sentence demanded by justice without complaint.
Specific Applications	The pastor-counselor, when dealing with a person struggling to grip scriptural principles of justice, need only furnish basic examples of when justice is not executed. Concocting an anecdote or the use of a real-life illustration is helpful when a person guilty of robbery or murder is released on bail with no just sentence, only later to repeat the same crime.
Homework	Assign the person struggling with a biblical sense of justice to read the prohibitions listed in the second table of the Ten Commandments, and then ask them what they think would constitute a just punishment for violating them—say for theft, adultery, or lying. Establishing a biblical approach to justice is critical to helping the abused and abusers process the entire issue according to the

ethic of the gospel.

CHAPTER 4

The Command for CONFESSION: The Penitent's Song of Sorrow

"There may be some sins of which a man cannot speak, but there is no sin which the blood of Christ cannot wash away."
C.H. Spurgeon

"I acknowledged my sin to You, and my iniquity I did not hide; I said, "I will confess my transgressions to the LORD"; And You forgave the guilt of my sin. Selah." (Ps 32:5)

"Confess your sins to one another . . . so that you may be healed." (Jas 5:16)

When the words needed to sufficiently capture the ugly enormity of our sin elude us, the sacrifice of Christ is still all-sufficient. However, despite being insufficiently articulate in the conscience-stifling face of our sinful disgrace, our confession must find a voice. This is precisely the meaning behind the New Testament word and concept for confession. It is the combination of two Greek words which, when put together, simply mean, "to say the same thing." However, that begs the question of saying the same thing as "what" or saying the same things as "who"? To be true to its basic word construct and meaning, confession is an act where we say the same thing about our sin as does the Scripture; and since God is the author of Scripture, we say the same thing about our sin as God says. As an example, in practical terms, it means we don't describe an intentional falsehood as a "little white lie," but as an intentional violation of the ninth commandment in the decalogue—"You shall not bear false witness against your neighbor" (Exod 20:16). We call our sin exactly what God calls it and no less.

For $13.99, you can purchase from Walmart a 24x20 picture placarding the saying of Mormon Lawyer, James E. Faust: "When we tell little white lies, we become progressively color-blind. It is better to remain silent than to mislead." While somewhat insightful, a statement more consistent with the meaning of true confession would affirm that little white lies paint a verbal picture of our sins with such bland and indistinct hues that the sharp lines of truth are virtually erased. "Lying lips are an abomination to the LORD" (Prov 12:22). Further, silence is never advisable, being totally antithetical to the kind of biblical confession of sin embedded in the meaning of the word. Verbal confession of sin is the only thing that will put us on the straight road to forgiveness and healing. Silence is never better! Silence is sin!

Both outright denials of sin and the self-deceptive sugarcoating of sin prevent the only God-given pathway to true forgiveness. This is true in every case of sin regardless of the extent to which it does or does not plunge into the depths of the most deplorable of sins. Of all the sins that are most likely to be followed by lies and grand cover-ups, sexual sins of fornication and especially gross sexual misconduct are at the top. Sexual abuse cases, because of the degree to which the guilty are branded by all people as the lowest and most disgusting of all sinners, puts the tendency to lie and deny on a kind of satanic set of spiritual-numbing steroids. That said, the only unforgiveable sin is blasphemy of the Holy Spirit (Mark 3:28). The sin, however, which will damn far more people than blasphemy of the Holy Spirit is the impenitence that refuses to admit and confess sin: "The only unforgivable sin is the impenitence that justifies sin and opposes the purifying mercies of God in Christ."[1]

One of the proverbs, in the most graphically picturesque way possible, makes the point unmistakable: "This is the way of an adulterous woman: She eats and wipes her mouth, and says, 'I have done no wrong'" (Prov 30:20). The illustrative picture in this proverb is not primarily pointing to a case of sexual indiscretion, but to the unwillingness to admit and confess the sin, which prevented any chance of forgiveness. Let your mind absorb the picture. The "eating" and "wiping of the mouth" are

[1] David Powlison, "Making All Things New: Restoring Pure Joy to the Sexually Broken (Part 1)," *Christian Counseling and Educational Foundation* (CCEF), May 17, 2010, https://www.ccef.org/making-all-things-new-restoring-pure-joy-sexually-broken/. This article appeared as a chapter in the book *Sex and the Supremacy of Christ*, edited by John Piper and Justin Taylor, and published in 2005 by Crossway Books.

metaphors meant to suggest unmannerly, rude, and indulgent behavior expressing itself in the most grotesque way. Like the stereotypical picture of a Nordic Viking stuffing his face with a greasy leg of lamb, belching and guzzling wine while it drips down his beard, it is the picture of a consummate slob. The proverbial illustration is perfectly suited to depict a woman, not just sadly falling to adultery in an unguarded moment but embracing it with brazen impenitence and high-handed impunity. Beyond the infidelity, for which many have been guilty and then forgiven, this is what made the woman so completely repulsive. The primary lesson of the brief proverb is that the impenitent denial of sin is abhorrent to God. Consequently, as we move more specifically to a biblical confession of sin in cases of sexual abuse, only a truly genuine confession will suffice as a means of properly dealing with it.

Confession of sin is by no means unique to biblical Christianity. Everybody in the world has some notion and concept of the need for confession of sin. The reality of hurting other people by our actions and being hurt by the actions of others is woven into the human dilemma. Everyone needs, at one time or another, to be the guilty confessor and at other times the one receiving a confession from another. At times, because we are the offending party, we must confess to others and ask for their forgiveness. At other times in life, we become the person to whom another is confessing. We need to extend to them forgiveness. The world's concept of confession, however, is utterly destitute of the real genius behind forgiveness. In fact, it is only the distinctly Christian concept of confession and forgiveness as unfolded in the Bible that gets it right. It is the ethic of the gospel that places it on an altogether different foundation and therefore takes it to an altogether higher level. The view of all other world religions outside of Christianity and all humanly conceived ideas of confession show how fundamentally different are their views. Mahatma Gandhi is noted for what is regarded to be a nearly clairvoyant and otherworldly statement on confession. Gandhi said, "Confession of errors is like a broom which sweeps away the dirt and leaves the surface brighter and clearer. I feel stronger for confession."

The weakness of this statement is quite profound; precisely because the confession does not identify an object of confession. It is totally subjective implying that the sum-total benefit of confession is to the person guilty of sin and thus needing to confess. While any Christian will admit that confession has a healing effect, it simply is not the act of confession alone that effects forgiveness and meets the requirements of biblical confession. Gandhi's notion suggests that the sheer discipline and act of confession involves a kind of catharsis where the act of confession itself heals and boosts the strength of the inner person. But what is it in the Christian conception of confession that effectively "sweeps away the dirt and leaves the surface brighter and clearer"? It is solely that a provision completely outside of those confessing sin was made by Jesus when He voluntarily took on Himself the just payment for our sins. The confession of sin is simply the hand that stretches to reach the provision already made. The hands that reach are faith and the object of our confession, Almighty God, can extend forgiveness because the work of salvation was finished on the cross. Indeed, "the blood of Jesus His Son cleanses us from all sin" (1 John 1:7). The power of confession is not in the act of confession. The power of confession is in the act of atonement received as a free gift, not as a work. No act of confession, regardless of how earnestly it pleads or how long it agonizes can bring about cleansing. Mere confession, directed to anything or anyone other than the one and only sacrifice made for sin, is like jumping into the deep end of a pool without water and hoping we'll be washed on the way to the bottom.

Dorothy Dix, the pen name adopted by American journalist and columnist, Elizabeth Meriwether Gilmer, reflects one version of the best that humanly conceived ideas can conclude about confession. She is regarded to be the forerunner of today's popular advice columnists, and at the height of her popularity, was the highest paid and most widely read female journalist in America. Dix said of confession, "Confession is always weakness. The grave soul keeps its own secrets and takes its own punishment in silence."[2] If the biblical teaching is true and the meaning inherent in the word confession accurate, her definition is prophetic. Indeed, the silent soul that regards confession as weakness most certainly keeps its own secrets and takes its own punishment in silence. It takes its punishment in eternity without the chance to ever purge its secrets by confession.

---

[2] Elizabeth Meriwether Gilmer (Dorothy Dix), *Her Book: Every-Day Help For Every-Day People* (New York City: Funk and Wagnalls, 1927).

THE COMMAND FOR CONFESSION

The gospel of Jesus Christ infinitely transcends all such concepts of confession and forgiveness. The gospel of Christ does this because it alone provides the unfailing basis on which sin can be 1) confessed to the person offended, 2) forgiven by the offended person, and 3) entirely removed by the joint act of the offender confessing and the offended forgiving. The Scripture teaches us that for God to provide forgiveness to sinful men, He, of necessity, had to legally charge the guilt of our sin to Christ on the cross. This imputation of man's guilt to the sinless and innocent lamb of God is the reason He died. In so doing, Jesus quite literally removed and took out of the way the very thing that separated us and estranged us from God—

> When you were dead in your transgressions and the uncircumcision of your flesh, He made you alive together with Him, having forgiven us all our transgressions, having canceled out the certificate of debt consisting of decrees against us, which was hostile to us; and **He has taken it out of the way**, having nailed it to the cross (Col 2:13–14).

What Jesus nailed to the cross and took out of the way were the sins of men that totally estrange us and alienate us from God. By this act of sacrificial love, the Lord Jesus Christ provided the just payment for sin. When a person admits and confesses their sin to God, they have met the only condition required (along with faith in Christ) for their sins to be effectually removed and forgiven. It is a faith in the work of Christ who died for our sins and rose again from the dead to save us. When a man receives the free offer of such saving forgiveness and begins to realize the sheer enormity of the sins God has forgiven him, it is a joyous delight to forgive others of their sins against him. In fact, the parable of the King settling financial debts with his servants in Matthew 18 depicts our sins against God to be infinitely greater than any other person's sins against us. The only condition then, for a person to receive forgiveness for the sins they commit against another person, is to admit the sin, confess the sin, and ask forgiveness for the sin. God's forgiveness of the immensity of our sins is the gold-standard of forgiveness that enables us to freely forgive others their trespasses against us. While forgiveness is dealt with more specifically in the next section, as it relates to cases of sexual abuse, it is introduced here because forgiveness swings on the hinges of confession of sin.

If we say that we have no sin, we are deceiving ourselves and the truth is not in us. If we confess our sins, He is faithful and righteous to forgive us our sins and to cleanse us from all unrighteousness. If we say that we have not sinned, we make Him a liar and His word is not in us (1 John 1:8–10).

The reader cannot miss the three conditional sentences of 1 John 1:8–10 marked by the word, "if." All three of these conditional statements revolve around the need for a brute, no holds barred confession of sin. Inseparably united to these statements of confession or non-confession of sin is the promise of the forgiveness of sin or the obvious withholding of forgiveness, both conditioned on either the denial of sin or the confession of sin. The first conditional sentence indicates a denial of the pervasiveness of sin in our nature and involves a form of self-deception revealing a fundamental dishonesty with self (we are deceiving ourselves and the truth is not in us). The third conditional sentence is a denial that the person is guilty of any specific act of sin. When a person does this, since it is obvious that personal sin is unquestionable, it is tantamount to accusing God of dishonesty and reveals a total repudiation of Scripture (we make Him a liar and His word is not in us). In the second conditional sentence, located in the middle of the verses, the person is meeting the condition for forgiveness by admitting and saying the same thing about their sin as does Scripture and God. In this case, and only in this case, the person is promised to be completely absolved of their sin. The promise of forgiveness, when sin is confessed, is rooted in two attributes of God: 1) The faithfulness of God—He will always forgive our sin when confession is made and faith is placed in Christ, and 2) the justice of God—God is fair and executes a perfect justice to remove the guilt of our sin when confession is made.

This is one of the greatest promissory blessings given in all of Scripture. It promises by the oath of God's own mouth, upon confession, that our sin is totally forgiven. This promise is extensive and effects both objective forgiveness and a subjective cleansing. Objectively, our sin is removed from the very presence of God (He is faithful and righteous **to forgive** us our sins). Subjectively, upon confession, the individual is purified from the stain and pollution of sin (and **to cleanse us** from all unrighteousness). This brief overview of this *locus classicus* on the confession and forgiveness of sin well justifies our oft-used Christian adage—make sure you keep a short account of your sins! While this passage does not comprehensively exhaust the great threats to confession of sin, it does imply that there are a variety of things that constitute what might be called "the great enemies of biblical confession." These enemies work in general cases of sin to fiercely oppose confession. In cases of sexual abuse, however, such enemies work with an Armageddon-like-force in particularly defiant ways that mitigate against the confession of sin.

It is vitally important to identify these enemies of confession. As mentioned in the exposure section, the best-case scenario for confession of sin is when it is voluntarily offered by the person guilty of the sin against God and against another person. Since, however, confession of such deviant sins is often not voluntary, at least in the initial stages, this exposé of the enemies to confession will proceed on the assumption that the exposure of the sin of the sexual abuser is one in which their sin was discovered and brought to light by a person other than the abuser. Such a discovery of sin absolutely mandates a ***confrontation*** of the abuser. It is in observing the tendencies that typically characterize the reactions of abusers that reveal the enemies to confession. Again, these same tendencies are evidenced when less severe infractions require confrontation, but they are compounded exponentially when sexual abuse requires confrontation.

The Impulse to Run and Hide

When the full exposure of sin meets the need for full confession, a variety of sinful impulses emerge in the heart of the sinner. As was alluded to previously, the impulse to hide (a feature that wars against confession) is not unique to those who are caught red-handed in the worst of sins. It is a phenomenon experienced by all who have had their ugly sins exposed. It is a spiritual consequence of the fall of man in general and is easily detectable as a psychological response when deep shame accompanies the exposure of sin. The deeper the shame associated with the specific sin, the greater becomes the impulse to run and hide. A personal example from my youth will illustrate the point.

When I was in late elementary school, I took a peach from about a quarter of a bushel of peaches that my mother purchased and had forbidden all of us to take. I then lied about it. To extract a confession from the guilty party, my mother pressed me very hard about owning up to the crime. She knew me well enough to conclude that I, among my siblings, was the most likely to be guilty. Yes, I was a wretch of a sinner even before I was a teenager and confession of sin did not come naturally. The worst part of the episode was that I swore to God on my mother's life that I did not take the peach. She left it at that. God, however, in the voice of my conscience, would not leave it at that. I had taken swearing to God on my mother's life so literally that I sincerely thought my lie required God to kill my mother. I was so guilty and afraid that it took me very little time to go back to my mother and confess I had taken (really stolen) the peach. Much to my delight, my mom exacted no further punishment whatsoever. I think she must have realized I had suffered enough from the lie.

As I look back at it now, I laugh it off as the antics and stupidity of an immature and unenlightened youth. But at that time, the searing pangs of conscience were not funny at all. They worked on me like a self-induced death sentence. The only way to relieve my very real agony was by true confession. But it was a confession aimed at self-preservation rather than offered to the God against whom I had sinned so egregiously. My mother, an unbeliever at that time, exposed the shame of my spiritual nakedness in an unforgettable way. As a Christian now for over four decades and a trained minister of the gospel, it makes me recall a verse I have seen play out many times in the lives of people when "caught in a transgression" (Gal 6:1). Hebrews 4:12–13 tells us,

> For the word of God is living and active, sharper than any two-edged sword, piercing to the division of soul and of spirit, of joints and of marrow, and discerning the thoughts and intentions of the heart. And no creature is hidden from his sight, but all are **naked and exposed** to the eyes of him to whom we must give account.

Sadly, rather than leading us to repentance and confession, the exposure of sin incites natural sinful man to attempt to cover the shame of his nakedness. Even more unforgettable is the strong exhortation to being in a constant state of preparedness for the coming of the Lord. Revelation 16:15 states, "Behold, I am coming like a thief! Blessed is the one who stays awake, keeping his garments on, that he may not **go about naked and be seen exposed!**" When God exposes the shame of our nakedness by the revelation of sin that must be confronted, it is not an act of cruelty meant to produce unending embarrassment. It is meant to set into motion the healing effected by an unqualified confession of sin leading to absolute forgiveness. Upon true confession, which is the condition for forgiveness, as with my mom, God exacts no further payment!

People will sometimes spend many years trying to build a barrier to dealing with their sin by placing one rational block on top of another to shield them from having to deal with the sin head on. As Walter J. Chantry says, "Cover-up is the first instinct of a sinner whose evil deeds are about to be exposed."[3] In God's goodness and grace, He may bring down the elaborate building of rationalization erected to conceal the sin. While all people do not sin to the same degree and excess, we all nevertheless sin. We can all understand the sinful inclination to respond in pride and rationalization to cover the shame of our own sin. We have all done this to one degree or another, and the reason is pointed out clearly in Scripture. When Proverbs 28:13 says that a person who covers their sin will not prosper, it is implying there is a rather powerful sinful tendency to bury our sins beneath the soil of recognition. When John 3:19–20 says

---

[3] Walter J. Chantry, *David: Man of Prayer, Man of War* (Edinburgh, UK: The Banner of Truth Trust, 2015).

that sinful man's natural attraction to spiritual darkness sends him into hiding when his sin is confronted, it is explicitly stating the overwhelming urge to hide rather than confess.

How many times in the history of humanity has a murderer attempted to cover their sin by taking the dead body into some dense and remote forest and burying it? You can imagine their thought process. Guilty, shamed beyond imagination, and fearful of being found out, they dig frantically, throw the body into the deep hole, and cover it with layer after layer of dirt, thinking *surely no one will ever discover the body of this evidence.* The attempt is futile. Like Rodion Raskolnikov in Fyodor Dostoevsky's *Crime and Punishment*, his guilt betrayed him and compelled his confession. The excruciating mental anguish and paranoia that resulted from his murder of the unscrupulous pawnbroker and his subsequent attempt to cover it up could only be resolved by confession. "I acknowledged my sin to You, and my iniquity I did not hide; I said, 'I will confess my transgressions to the LORD'; And You forgave the guilt of my sin. Selah" (Ps 32:5).

The First Response Phenomenon

On the occasions in pastoral ministry when serious cases of sin compel a pastor to confront a person in the face of clear and obvious guilt, a rather interesting phenomenon occurs. The initial reaction to the allegation that they have sinned and must deal with it in a biblical manner can provoke a very proud, defensive, and elusive reaction. However, people who are genuinely converted and genuinely desire to honor God will often come back later with an altogether different spirit. They simply needed time to go away and deal with their sin in the presence of God and no other human. Given the time to consider the unmasked reality of their sin and the way in which it hurt others and dishonored the Lord, they will bow their wills, admit, confess, and seek forgiveness for their sin.

Like our original parents, we hear "the sound of the LORD God walking in the garden in the cool of the day," and just like Adam and Eve, we hide ourselves among the trees of denial, embarrassment, and shame. But later, and by the grace of God, we hear the sweet and inquiring voice of the Lord. "Then the LORD God called to the man, and said to him, 'Where are you?' He said, 'I heard the sound of You in the garden, and I was afraid because I was naked; so I hid myself'" (Gen 3:9–10). Despite our attempts to camouflage our sins, His voice calls us out of the hidden haunts of sin where we have resorted and invites us to look to the Savior whose blood was shed for our sins and to be clothed in the robes of His pure white righteousness. His voice calls us to confession, but it doesn't always come immediately and can take time!

While serving at Shaw Air Force Base in the early 1980s, a lieutenant colonel related a very interesting personal story. While mowing his lawn, he slipped on a hilly section of his yard and his foot went underneath the housing of the lawnmower. The spinning blade cut off his big toe. As an instinctual act of self-deception, he got right back up and kept mowing the lawn as if to tell himself nothing was wrong. It was a first response phenomenon, but it could not conceal the traumatic injury his foot suffered. It was not until the bloody stump left him limping and with no other alternative that he was ready to admit he was seriously wounded. Only then did he seek the medical help needed to suture his lacerated foot. It is true that the ugliest of sins can turn our faces away from the reality that we are hemorrhaging spiritually. While it may take us some time to focus on the full extent of our sinful wound and to feel the acute agony, only an unqualified confession of sin can dress it with the spiritual bandage sufficient to heal the festering wound. We must confess our sin! Apart from that initial move on the part of the offender to completely confess, forgiveness, while it can be offered, cannot be granted. "But when he came to his senses, he said . . . 'I will get up and go to my father, and will say to him, "Father, I have sinned against heaven, and in your sight; I am no longer worthy to be called your son"'" (Luke 15:17–19).

The Royal Cover-Up

Sinful man is quite clever at masking their sins. We are all naturally doctors of self-deceit. The greater the sin, the more ingenious become our efforts at cover-up. The lies to cover lies becomes a thicket where the manufacturer of the lies cannot even avoid the entanglements. "O, what a tangled web we weave when first we practice to deceive!" Nowhere is this tendency greater than in cases of sexual infidelity. So great is the betrayal and so enormous the searing guilt that the most basic fallen spiritual instinct of self-preservation kicks into gear full force and the attempt to cover up begins. King David, the sweet Psalmist of Israel, and the man after God's own heart, is singularly the most infamous example of this truth.

The sad saga of David's sin with Bathsheba and the cascading waterfall of sinful consequences that followed it are the stuff of biblical legend—renowned and remarkable because of its historical truth. Second Samuel 11–12 are the narrative chapters that record the historical details of David's fall. Psalm 32, one of the six penitential psalms, records David's confession after the whole ordeal worked in him a profound repentance and confession. His repentance and confession were every bit as monumental as was his sin!

> When I kept silent about my sin, my body wasted away Through my groaning all day long. For day and night Your hand was heavy upon me; My vitality was drained away as with the fever heat of summer. Selah. I acknowledged my sin to You, and my iniquity I did not hide; I said, "I will confess my transgressions to the LORD"; And You forgave the guilt of my sin. Selah (Ps 32:3–5).

The power of sin that works so feverishly against true confession of sin is skillfully sketched out in this psalm. The opening words to this paragraph, "When I kept silent about my sin," are a brief window into a period of David's life in which he was impenitent and unwilling (or unready) to admit and confess his sin. There are four statements in this psalm that indicate, before David confessed and received forgiveness for his sin, how he handled it: 1) He kept silent about his sin; 2) He did not acknowledge his sin; 3) He attempted to keep his sin hidden; and 4) He did not confess his sin. Further, the full biblical sketch of his sin involved, at the very least, the following things: covetousness, idolatry, adultery, lying, murder, and hypocrisy. From the time he committed adultery, later involving the murder of Uriah the Hittite, to the time when the prophet Nathan confronted David with the enormity of his sin and guilt, he had gone nine long months with the poison of his sin wreaking deadly effects on his body and soul.

During the nine-month period he "kept silent" and allowed all these sins to remain bottled up inside of him, he was absolutely tortured in soul, mind, and body ("My body wasted away through my groaning all day long. For day and night Your hand was heavy upon me; My vitality was drained away as with the fever heat of summer").

It was not until God allowed the home-spun parable of the prophet Nathan to expose David's wickedness and hypocrisy that he came to his senses. It was not until the blunt candor of the prophet's convicting words, "you are the man" (2 Sam 12:7), that David finally broke under the weight of his sin. It was not until the undeniable verdict of his awful guilt crashed with tidal force onto his consciousness that he finally admitted and confessed, "I have sinned against the LORD" (2 Sam 13:13). Only after a royal and sophisticated attempt to cover-up his sin did God, in His great love for David, perfectly orchestrate the events that would ultimately bring David to confession.

Cover-ups never work. They always fail. Yet cover-up is often viewed as the only alternative in the face of such disgusting sins. As William Wordsworth said, "From the body of one guilty deed a thousand ghostly fears and haunting thoughts proceed."[4] The impulse to cover up is magnified a million times over when it is the guilty deeds of sexual abuse that require full admission. In his phenomenally insightful analysis of temptation, *Temptation Resisted and Repulsed*, John Owen discloses why the urge to cover up sin is so powerful—consequences!

> Men sometimes are carried into sin, just by the love of it, but they often persist, and remain in it, because of the fear of the consequences that might follow repentance and full disclosure.[5]

Nevertheless, confession on the part of any abuser, preceded by a brute honesty about the nature of the sin, is the only hope. Forgiveness swings on the hinges of confession. "If You, LORD, should mark iniquities, O Lord, who could stand? But there is forgiveness with You, that You may be feared" (Ps 130:3–4). Abusers need to fear that unless they admit, confess, and repent of such sins, that the spiritual pangs of a tormented conscience in

---

[4] William Wordsworth, *The Complete Poetical Works of William Wordsworth: Together with a Description of the Country of the Lakes in the North of England* (Sterling Ford, UK: Wentworth Press, 2016), 239.

[5] John Owen, *Temptation: Resisted and Repulsed*, Edited by Richard Rushing (Edinburgh, UK: Banner of Truth Trust, 2012), 23.

this life are but a foretaste of the whole-person torment they will feel eternally.

The impact David felt while he remained impenitent and unwilling to confess his sin was a brief period when measured against his entire life. Those who live an entire life of impenitence will experience, over the duration of eternity in hell, an assault on their soul, mind, and body infinitely greater than did David. David's sorrow, grief, and acute pain, when he remained impenitent, is a temporary miniature of the sorrow, grief, and pain that will be felt infinitely by those who live all their life and then die in impenitence. This is true of all impenitent sinners!

> For I know [acknowledge] my transgressions, and my sin is ever before me. Against You, You only, I have sinned and done what is evil in Your sight, so that You are justified when You speak and blameless when You judge (Ps 51:3–4).

Hardened or Humbled: The Two Polar Responses

Any effort to bring those guilty of sin to confession must be initiated by confrontation, but confrontation is very uncomfortable. Even when sinful offenses that must be confronted do not rise to the level of abuse, it is immensely difficult for both the person confronting as well as the person being confronted. The entire process may eventually produce a response that resolves the issue of sin, but this never happens apart from the grace of God, the wise application of Scripture, and the operation of the Holy Spirit. Working toward biblical resolution is the clear goal, but it involves a process where the outcome is determined by many variables and is not always certain. There is, however, one common denominator in every case where sin must be confronted—conflict. Due to the tenacity of Satan and the incredible degree of human sinfulness and pride, attempting to scripturally resolve serious conflicts is met by numerous stereotypical responses. Sande and Johnson write,

> There are three basic ways people respond to conflict. We choose to escape, attack, or make peace. . . . When conflict happens, the escaper focuses on running. The attacker aims at winning. The peacemaker's goal is reconciling. Escape responses are usually peace-faking, trying to make things look good even when they aren't. Attack responses are peace-breaking, sacrificing people and peace to get what we want. Peacemaking applies the gospel and God's principles for problem solving to everyday life.[6]

When sin severely disrupts otherwise good relationships, the negative tendencies to escape and attack can dictate the reactions of both the offender and the offended. However, if we shift our attention more narrowly to some very typical responses on the part of guilty people when confronted, one of two things normally happen. They are either *humbled* in light of the guilt of

---

[6] Ken Sande and Kevin Johnson, *Resolving Everyday Conflict* (Grand Rapids: Baker Books, 2011), 37, 39, 41, 43.

their sin or they are *hardened* when made to confront their sin. As mentioned above, a humble response may require some time, but beyond the reasonable allowance of time, the response to confrontation does not vary widely at all and seems to take place between one of these two polar responses: either humbling or hardening.

In any case involving serious sin, a biblical approach confronts the person along the lines of the three component parts of the human personality: intellect, emotion, and will. *Intellectually*, the reality of their sin is enlightened so that they mentally visualize and grip the significance of what they have done. But awareness of sin on the intellectual level alone does not necessarily lead to admission, repentance, and confession. *Emotionally*, they may react in a very volatile fashion. They may become very agitated and angry. Or they may react with an emotional sorrow that leaves them on the floor in a puddle of regret. The angry response is certainly not repentance, but neither is the tearful response when the confession is nothing more than mere regret.

> See to it that no one comes short of the grace of God; . . . that there be no immoral or godless person like Esau, who sold his own birthright for a single meal. For you know that even afterwards, when he desired to inherit the blessing, he was rejected, for he found no place for repentance, though he sought for it with tears (Heb 12:15–17).

The third aspect of the human personality that is confronted is the *volitional* part of man—his will. It is at this level that the person chooses to either harden or humble themselves in the scriptural light of their sinful conduct. When the intellect cannot deny the truthful reality of sin and the emotion is deeply constrained by the pain of sin, the volitional part of man, of necessity, will respond. The willful reaction will hopefully be humble, but it may be hardened. In a sense, sin has a mind of its own and often will not respond in rational ways. When the sin is of a vile, sexual nature and deeply entrenched, it requires a great deal of God's grace along with skillful wisdom on the part of the confronter to encourage the guilty to be forthcoming with an honest admission and repentant confession of their sin. The apostle Paul's classic pastoral advice to Timothy reveals why bringing such persons to confession is so tenuous—

> The Lord's bond-servant must not be quarrelsome, but be kind to all, able to teach, patient when wronged, with gentleness correcting those who are in opposition, if perhaps God may grant them repentance leading to the knowledge of the truth, and they may come to their **senses** and escape from the **snare** of the devil, having been held **captive** by him to do his will (2 Tim 2:24–26).

The grip that sin can have on a man, even a confessing Christian man, is powerful in the extreme. When Paul uses the expression, "that they may come to [recover] their senses," he uses a word directly related to the use of wine, and more particularly, the worst effects that wine can have upon a person. What this means is that Satan acts upon the soul and spirit of men like alcohol and narcotics act upon the mind and body of a man. The words, "from the snare of the devil," refer to the trigger stick that sets off an animal trap and drops a cage on them. It insinuates that sin can so thoroughly ensnare a person that they are completely powerless to set themselves free, even though it is a snare from which God wants them to escape. The words, "having been held captive by him to do his will," is a military term that suggests how an enemy carries a person off as a captive of war. The effect is that the person in sin is completely impotent to escape on their own and are under a force that handcuffs them. They are bound to do Satan's bidding (held captive by him to do his will).

Consequently, egregious sins of the flesh are particularly capable of hardening people because Satan's power over them acts like a poison that tricks and imprisons them. Confrontation of such people is often a complicated attempt to unravel a rather stubborn three-chord knot. It is this satanic work that underlies a hardened will that becomes implacable, unrepentant, and completely unwilling to confess. There is no certainty whatsoever when people are so bound in sin that they will come clean with God. This is exactly why Paul advises a humble and uncontentious pastoral approach when confronting people in opposition. It is the un-quarrelsome, instructive, patient, gentle approach that is most likely to bring a person to acknowledgement of their sin (if perhaps God will grant them repentance leading to the knowledge of truth).

The hardening of our hearts when confronted with sin is something with which we all must be on guard because it is something with which we all struggle. The reason why confrontation can meet with such a hardened response rather than a humble response, is because it shines a massive light directly onto the sin, and in the process, directly exposes the sinfulness of the person. This can be embarrassing to the point of utter humiliation because it forces the person to look at themselves in the mirror of God's Word. It forces them to take off the rose-tinted glasses of sinful excuses and rationalization and to look at themselves as they are in all their hideous ugliness. It forces them to what enlightenment philosopher Immanuel Kant described as the "hard descent into the Hell of self-knowledge." The work of God through Scripture, by means of those who must confront us with our sin, forces us to look directly into the hell of our own heart. When it works according to God's intention, it brings deep sorrow and an unequivocal confession of our sin. It leads us to say about our sin the same thing God says about it. It leads us to confess!

If, because of our sin, God labels us as fornicators, idolaters, adulterers, effeminate, homosexuals, thieves, covetous, drunkards, revilers, or swindlers, true confession will say the same thing and label it exactly as does He. We will confess our sins! Such unreserved confession becomes the surest evidence of genuine sorrow for our sin and makes the best argument possible that we desire change and genuine transformation. "Such were some of you; but you were washed, but you were sanctified, but you were justified in the name of the Lord Jesus Christ and in the Spirit of our God" (1 Cor 6:9–10). Divine forgiveness is never applied apart from genuine confession. By the grace of God, the confrontation of the guilty person will lead to their confession, which, because of the sufficiency of Christ's atonement, engages the wheels of forgiveness provided by Christ. Once the genuine wheels of confession are moving, it then confronts the offended person (even the abused) with the biblical obligation to forgive as much as the offending person was confronted with their obligation to confess!

	Points of Practical Pastoral Wisdom
Primary Goal	In the third stage of applying the ethic of the gospel to cases of sexual abuse the pastor-counselor should facilitate genuine confession of sin by unveiling all its benefits.
Real Life Examples	My father, when he was very elderly, once got very angry with my wife, blaming her, and verbally yelling at her for blocking his car in the driveway. It was another person's car, so it was outrageously inappropriate and unfair. I knew I had to speak with him. But that became unnecessary as the next morning he came to her and offered the most humble and heartfelt apology, admitting his sin, saying it was totally inexcusable, and asking her to forgive him. She

THE COMMAND FOR CONFESSION

	embraced him and gladly forgave him. I will always remember it as the most biblical example of confession I ever witnessed.
Vital Questions	Do you understand the importance of confession of sin as taught in the Bible? Have you ever confessed specific sins to God? Have you ever confessed specific sins to other people against whom you have sinned? How would you define confession of sin? Do you think forgiveness of sin is conditioned on confession?
Typical Counselee Responses	Confession of sin often comes piece meal, a little bit at a time. Outright denial of clear sin, sugarcoating sin, masking it, and speaking of it in broad generalities are typical responses that fall short of the specific confession needed to move toward forgiveness.
Specific Applications	Go over obstacles of confession of sin such as: 1) Refusing complete acknowledgment of sin to self, which is internal and often involves self-humiliation or self-embarrassment. 2) Refusing unqualified admission to others, which is external and overcomes self-humiliation. 3) Refusal to make a verbal request for forgiveness that entails the total exposure of personal guilt.

Homework	Since 1 John 1:8-10 is such a classic New Testament commentary on confession of sin, require that the person read over it multiple times, take notes about the key ideas, and then explain how they interpret and understand its significance. Afterward, ask if they feel they have applied the teaching to their own life.

CHAPTER 5

The Glory of FORGIVENESS: Doing with the Sins of Others as God Has Done with Ours

"He has not dealt with us according to our sin, nor rewarded us according to our iniquities." (Ps 103:10)

"Be kind to one another, tender-hearted, forgiving each other, just as God in Christ also has forgiven you." (Eph 4:32)

"If I cast up a confessed, repented, and forsaken sin against another, and allow my remembrance of that sin to colour my thinking and feed my suspicions, then I know nothing of Calvary's love."
—Amy Carmichael

The astounding observation made by Amy Carmichael is easy to miss, or at least to interpret it opposite of the way she intended. Her confession that a wrong sense of forgiveness of sins indicates the possibility of knowing "nothing of Calvary's love," is not pointing to a person having granted forgiveness to another and then struggling with recalling the offense back to mind. She is not describing a person struggling to persist in forgiving a person they have already forgiven. No! She is observing that when a person who is guilty of sinning against another, however grievously, recalls to mind and memory a sin for which they have already confessed and been forgiven; it is they who know nothing of Calvary's love. Wow!

This reminds me of my seminary days when one of the favored professors would make soul-staggering comments about the full implications of the blessings of the gospel of Christ. To some, his insightful comments seemed scandalous. To others, they opened a window into a little piece of heaven and gave us a glimpse of the glory of all that God had accomplished for us through the cross-work of His Son. He would say on the subject of forgiveness, "when you re-confess to God a sin you have already confessed, God says, 'I don't know what you're talking about.'" He would cite Hebrews 10:17 as the basis for his comment: "AND THEIR SINS AND THEIR LAWLESS DEEDS I WILL REMEMBER NO MORE." Get it reader, missing God's mark and transgressing the clearly-defined boundaries prescribed by His laws are forgiven under the New Covenant. Our sins, when the original sense of the words in Hebrews 10:17 is drawn out, remain no longer in the mind of God. They are removed and there is nothing left to squeeze out of them. Once forgiven, the total removal of the sin erases it from the mind and memory of God; so why bring it up again? Sins forgiven are sins forgotten. This is the glory of forgiveness!

I, even I, am the one who wipes out your transgressions for My own sake, and I will not remember your sins (Isa 43:25).

I have wiped out your transgressions like a thick cloud and your sins like a heavy mist (Isa 44:22).

Pushed to The Limits

The divine forgiveness of the enormity of man's sin is glorious indeed, but when the sins of men against fellow man plummet to unfathomable depths of depravity, it demands a level of forgiveness impossible to achieve by human power alone. Let's face it, all sin is not equal in either degree or in the extent to which it offends and causes another person to stumble. Yes, all sin is equal in its power to condemn men before a holy God on the vertical level. "For whoever keeps the whole law and yet stumbles in one point, he has become guilty of all" (Jas 2:10). But all sin does not rise to the same level of horror on the human to human, horizontal level. A child who works on a model airplane at an oak kitchen table in disregard of his parent's explicit commands not to do so and ruins a section of the table surface by spilling glue on it will likely find himself in a whole heap of trouble. But Stalin's systematic starvation of twenty million peasants rises to an altogether higher level. If the young boy who disobeyed his parent's prohibition remains impenitent for the duration of his life regarding his general problem with sin and never seeks forgiveness, he will perish. Both he and Stalin have incurred a guilt sufficient to condemn them. But the extent of Stalin's sin on a human level clearly indicates he has amassed a degree of criminality far in excess; and it would appear he will receive a greater severity of judgement. Jesus Himself seems to suggest this. He taught that those guilty of spurning the highest degrees of privileged revelation are liable to a more severe degree of punishment: "Nevertheless, I say unto you, it will be more tolerable for Tyre and Sidon than for you" (Luke 11:22).

People who are part of orchestrating genocide or a person guilty of serial killings are not nightmarish hypotheticals dreamed up in the imaginative mind of an author of horror novels. They represent part of real-world examples of human beings whose actions defy all explanations, other than mankind is horribly twisted and depraved beyond imagination. Under certain formative influences, conditions, and impulses set aflame by Satan, men may commit unspeakable atrocities against other people. Sexual abuse, while all cases do not rise to the same level of offense or degree of injury, is such a sin. In such cases, the limits of forgiveness can get pushed to the extreme and tested far beyond what any of us might wish. This is not to say that the requirement and obligation to forgive according to the ethic of the gospel is lessened in cases of gross sin; it is simply admitting to the reality that the most awful sins that might be described as a sin against humanity (or sins against the dignity of another person) stretch our human capacity for forgiveness to extreme limits.

I do not write as a mere theoretician who enjoys a good soul-teaser that titillates the inquiring mind with eerie, unanswerable enigmas that belong in a test laboratory—like the proverbial theologian enamored with how many angels can dance on the head of a needle. No, not at all! The subject hits as close to home as I could ever wish. Having done crisis-counseling for many years, the array of sick and disgusting ways that humans sin against one another, quite literally, defies description. Can such sins ever be forgiven? In over twenty-nine years of gospel ministry pastoring relatively small churches, I have counseled people and couples in nearly every type of scenario the mind can imagine. I have been compelled, by the genius of the Christian gospel, to counsel people who are the victims of disgustingly unthinkable offenses to forgive their offenders. I have done so on the sheer principles of biblical truth that I trust and am persuaded reflect the mind and will of God. I have personally been the object of gossip, false accusations, scandalous lies, and defamation of my character. Welcome to the gospel ministry that approximates in some small way an experience patterned after the life of Jesus. But being completely honest, the limits to which my need to forgive others have never been pushed anywhere near to the limits of those sexually abused or surviving members of a murdered family victim.

In 2008, Kimberly Clark Saenz, now known as the infamous Nightmare Nurse, ruthlessly murdered five patients at

---

[1] Jessica Cooley, "Angelina County Jury Finds Saenz Guilty of Killing Patients at DaVita by Injecting Dialysis Lines with Bleach," *Lufkin News*, March 30, 2012. http://lufkindailynews.com/news/local/article_f7afb142-7ad9-11e1-90d7-001a4bcf887a.html.

the busiest dialysis clinic in Lufkin, TX.[1] Her chosen method of murder was to inject bleach into the kidney dialysis tubing of five patients. The five murder victims were Clara Strange, Thelma Metcalf, Garlin Kelley, Cora Bryant, and Opal Few.[20] On April 2, 2012, the Angelina County jury sentenced Saenz to life in prison with no eligibility for parole for one count of capital murder each for the five patients who died. She was also charged with aggravated assault against five other patients who were allegedly injected with bleach but survived. When we hear of such sinful actions, we are absolutely repulsed and feel as if such a thing cannot be true and that we must be living within some bloody, fictitious horror film. These kinds of atrocities push the limits of forgiveness to the extreme. The daughter of one of the murder victims, commented—

> "How can someone that sick walk around and appear to be a normal person?" said Linda Few, whose mother, Opal, was among the five who died. "This many people? It's blowing my mind. I mean, we live in Lufkin."[2]

Is there an answer to why people do things that simply "blow the mind"? Is there some explanation for such atrocities? The answer is an emphatic yes! The answer is in the consistent and overwhelming evidence presented in Scripture and running all the way from Genesis to Revelation. We are not four chapters

---

[2] Ryan Smith, "Nightmare Nurse: Poisonous Injections Could Net Death Penalty," *CBS News*, July 16, 2009, https://www.cbsnews.com/news/nightmare-nurse-poisonous-injections-could-net-death-penalty/.

into the biblical record in Genesis that the first son to ever live and the first older brother to join in a sibling relationship stretches out a knife that cuts the throat of his little brother. The first murder in the Bible! The guilt of shedding his brother's blood is personified in the biblical story when God Himself confronts Cain and asks him, "What have you done? The voice of your brother's blood is crying to Me from the ground" (Gen 4:10). The murder was an outrage first and foremost to God. Could it ever be forgiven?

From the story of Cain and Abel forward, the biblical record is quite literally an enormous case file that catalogues the near infinite amount of sin committed by men against their fellow man, and more significantly, against God. Some of the general categories into which this catalogue of sins fall include child sacrifice (2 Chron 33:6; Ps. 106:36–37), incest (Gen 19:30–38; Lev 18:6), consulting with the dead—necromancy (Lev 19:26; Deut 18:10; Gal 5:19–20; Acts 19:19), gross oppression and social injustice (Eccl 5:8), adultery (Exod 20:14; Matt 5:29; Eph 5:3), lying (Exod 20:16; Ps 5:9), homosexuality (Rom 1:26–28; 1 Cor 6:9; Lev.18:22), male and female prostitution (Prov 9:13–18; 1 Cor 6:9), bestiality—sexual intercourse with animals (Lev 18:23), and worst of all, blasphemy (Matt 12:31; Luke 12:10). Blasphemy is not just using the name of God along with a string of other expletives. Blasphemy is a sin where a person willfully defames the character of God by justifying wicked conduct in the name of God—conduct totally antithetical to God's character and will. This is far from a complete list.

To all this, it must be affirmed that the Bible never forbids that which is not within the realm of possibility. Furthermore, both the biblical record along with human experience proves that mankind can and does commit such sins. Again, can God ever forgive such an array of sins? Is there a provision for forgiveness, and is there a process where people guilty of the most heinous sins can appropriate that forgiveness to themselves? Yes, God has made a provision for forgiveness of sins through Christ bearing the guilt and condemnation of man's sin on the cross. The glory of forgiveness begins to emerge as we carefully and fully behold the extent to which God forgives us. His forgiveness of us becomes the standard for how we forgive others. And it must be restated, as hinted at earlier, that no sin of guilty men against other guilty men, no matter how atrocious, comes anywhere near our personal sin against an innocent and infinitely holy God. Before, however, answering more fully how such a provision applies in cases of sexual abuse, consider a specific case of immense offense against others freely forgiven when genuine repentance takes place.

One of the most notoriously wicked kings to ever sit on the throne of Judah was Manasseh. He ruled in the seventh century BC for fifty-five years during the single kingdom period (after the Northern ten tribes had already been subjugated by Assyria). King Manasseh absolutely polluted the nation with abominations that defy description. Under his influence, the nation engaged in Baal worship, sacred prostitution, and necromancy. He placed an idol directly in the temple (an Asherah pole) and showed rabid devotion to astrological bodies.

Ultimately, he sacrificed his own children to the cult of Moloch. The Old Testament history captures his entire reign with the following description—

> In both courts of the temple of the Lord, he built altars to all the starry hosts. He sacrificed his children in the fire in the Valley of Ben Hinnom, practiced divination and witchcraft, sought omens, and consulted mediums and spiritists. He did much evil in the eyes of the Lord, arousing his anger (2 Chron 33:5–6).

What if Manasseh repents? What if he admits, confesses his sin, and seeks forgiveness? Surely, no atonement can be made for him! Many have asked this question in cases of gross sin, where the sin is horrifically egregious and the fallout on others is catastrophic. What does God do when an offender, as the adage says, repents as profoundly as he sinned? The divine verdict when confession and repentance is genuinely evident is forgiveness and a restored relationship with Him.

> And when he [King Manasseh] was in distress, he entreated the favor of the LORD his God and humbled himself greatly before the God of his fathers. He prayed to him, and God was moved by his entreaty and heard his plea and brought him again to Jerusalem into his kingdom. Then Manasseh knew that the LORD was God (2 Chron 33:12–13).

Can God be "moved" by the entreaty of a sinner as abominably vile as Manasseh? I would have never thought so. But, alas, I am forgetting the gospel which is offered for sinners just like Manasseh, and just like me and just like you. No one ever comprehends the riches of the gospel until they comprehend the extent of their own depravity. Yes, we are all as depraved as Manasseh, and that is no overstatement at all. Our sin, in its visible manifestation, may be different than that of Manasseh or different from some other person, but it is equally excessive at its root, in our own hearts where every imaginable monster of sin prowls and roams. On the way to the glory of forgiveness, whether you're the offender needing forgiveness or the offended needing to forgive, a massive part of the genius of what enables Christians to forgive others is the realization of the depth and extent of your own depravity. Such a realization resists the temptation to compare our sins, which we believe to be lesser, with the sins of others which we believe to be greater. When the glory of gospel-based forgiveness begins to triumph in our experience, we find ourselves grieving primarily for the offenses we have given (especially against God), not the offenses we have received!

The Psychology of Control

Professional psychologists as well as trained clergy witness various post-assault attempts made by abuse victims to control the effects of the abuse and to control the abuser. For professing Christians who have been assaulted, they may initially offer to the offender forgiveness because the offender has genuinely repented, confessed, and sought forgiveness. Later, victims of abuse may attempt forms of control that bring into question the genuineness and extent of their forgiveness along the lines of the gospel. When unconditional forgiveness is granted by the person assaulted, the acceptance of that forgiveness by the guilty person greatly aids them in receiving the full sense of forgiveness as well as their own personal healing and transformation. We all know that this happens in a microcosm when a penitent person who has sinned willfully against God in some lesser egregious sexual sin receives God's free and gracious forgiveness upon admission, confession, and repentance of their sin. The assurance of God's full forgiveness, based on faith in the all-sufficient sacrifice of Christ and the assurance they have been forgiven by the person against whom they sinned, is critical to freeing them from the guilt of sin and the emotionally enslaving power of Satan. The same dynamic, when we understand the basis of forgiveness rooted in the gospel, should be applied equally in more severe cases of sexual sin, even cases of sexual abuse. Consequently, the freedom and peace of mind that comes to the innocent when they freely forgive those who are guilty of sinning against them is as critical to their overall wellbeing as being forgiven is to the guilty. This is the glory of forgiveness according to the ethic of the gospel!

Sadly however, when the assaulted person absolutely refuses to forgive or later withdraws the forgiveness, the non-forgiver becomes the slave and can remain in the same kind of stifling bondage experienced by an unrepentant abuser. The unwillingness to extend forgiveness in the same way God has extended it to them creates a festering bitterness and a bitterness that seeks to control the consequences meted out to the guilty. "See to it that no one comes short of the grace of God; that no root of bitterness springing up causes trouble, and by it many be defiled" (Heb 12:15). When this happens, they allow both Satan and their embittered feelings toward the perpetrator to maintain a suffocating power over their own well-being. Having been at an earlier time totally under the control of their perpetrator, the only seeming way to deal with it is by an attempt at control which takes on the form of withholding forgiveness or trying to be the administrator of their punishment. As a friend of mine, who was a victim of abuse himself, said—

> Hatred is not the flame to which if you get to close you may singe your clothing. You are like a gasoline-soaked rag that only needs a spark. Whatever pain you hope to render by hating someone who doesn't love, you won't. But what you will do is finish your abuser's work for them. Don't drown the hope of newness in Christ in rage. Don't rob your children and your spouse of yourself. Don't wait until that horrible day when you realize that the thief who stole the rest of your life was you. No matter how much your abuser took from you Christ has given you far more.

In addition, those who are victims of assault may try to dictate the responses and relationship of everyone else toward the person guilty of the sin. This, while understandable and from a practical standpoint may suggest that we allow a reasonable amount of time for the full implications of a gospel-driven forgiveness to be extended by the abused, is nonetheless a form of control.

On the clinical and psychological front, assault survivors experience Rape Trauma Syndrome (RTS), which is an aspect that becomes critical in understanding the impulse to control. The approach of the typical clinical psychologist is likely more mental health driven than spiritual health driven, which is the primary concern of the Christian approach. It goes without saying that clinical psychologists are concerned for the spiritual well-being of their patients and that a Christian counselor should be equally concerned for all aspects of the wellbeing of a victim of sexual abuse: physical, mental, psychological, and spiritual. All these elements are, at once, bound together inseparably because a proper biblical view of the total essence of the human being is that he is an inseparable union of body, soul, and spirit. That is to say that the part of man's being that is physical and material is inseparable from the part of his being that is psychological and spiritual. Strike the body and you strike the soul. Afflict the soul and you afflict the body. The primary difference between the clinical psychologist and the Christian counselor, particularly when dealing with the need for a victim of abuse to grant forgiveness to their assailant, is that the Christian counselor will believe with an unshakable conviction that the sufficiency of Scripture together with the ethic of forgiveness as unfolded in the gospel of Jesus Christ is the genius and most critical element in full recovery. Chantry writes,

Those who judge reality by empirical proofs only have, by their choice of epistemology, shut their eyes to a most significant aspect of true being. Science, devoted exclusively to empirical observations, has nothing whatsoever to contribute on the vast subject of the spiritual...It is absurd to speak of science investigating such a proposition; for science investigates only material cause and effect... The disposition and moods of human spirits are not influenced only by social and material environments; they are acted upon by divine and demonic spirits. Thus, all who labor to soothe the troubled spirits of men must be humbled. At times they are involved with spiritual powers not wholly subject to counseling, scientific analysis, or chemical manipulations.[3]

Despite a decidedly spiritual, gospel-based approach to counsel, it is an unarguable fact that victims of RTS also experience an accompanying Post-Traumatic Stress Disorder (PTSD). How horrifically sad that females and males alike would ever be subject to sexual offenses against their person that impact their lives like a war veteran who has been shell-shocked because explosives hit too close to their ears. The shock reverberates forever within their being. The lasting effects of sexual abuse, apart from the grace of God and the work of His gospel, are simply staggering. Consequently, the extent of the PTSD figures into the effort of the abused to control the outcome rather than

---

[3] Walter J. Chantry, *David: Man of Prayer, Man of War* (Edinburgh, UK: The Banner of Truth Trust, 2015), 19, 21.

trusting and following God's Word and the counsel He advises according to the ethic of the gospel. On PTSD, Chivers-Wilson writes,

> Cognitive factors play a large role in the onset, severity, and outcome of PTSD after sexual assault. . . . If the survivor of sexual assault believes that others have failed to react in a positive and supportive manner, there is a greater risk of PTSD. . . . Events perceived as uncontrollable are much more distressing than controllable events, therefore with uncontrollable events such as sexual assault, survivors will attempt to attribute blame to behavioral, dispositional or vicarious causes. . . . Vicarious control refers to the perception that some other person or entity had control over the occurrence of that event. Attributing blame in any of these ways focuses on the past and is associated with poorer outcomes in PTSD. To improve PTSD, treatment outcomes emphasis should be on controlling the present situation and what can be done about the impact of the event, rather than how it could have been avoided or can be avoided in the future."[4]

Adopting a biblical and gospel-driven ethic as the best way to helping victims of sexual abuse, recognizing the essential role that granting forgiveness plays in their own healing, is to avoid

[4] Kaitlin A. Chivers-Wilson, "Sexual Assault and Posttraumatic Stress Disorder: A Review of the Biological, Psychological and Sociological Factors and Treatments," *McGill Journal of Medicine*, July 2006, https://www.ncbi.nlm.nih.gov/pmc/articles/PMC2323517/.

the attempt to "control" everything around them and to let God be in control. Every Christian has faced difficult circumstances in which they soon realize they have absolutely no control over final outcomes, and they have no control over the actions and attitudes of others. The only thing under their control is themselves; yet even self-control, when circumstances reach unbearable levels, is impossible by human will and strength alone. Such circumstances are taught in Scripture to ultimately be under the control and sovereign providence of God, "having been predestined according to His purpose who works all things after the counsel of His will" (Eph 1:11). In God's economy, it is only the most excruciating circumstances that forge in us the faith-driven approach to face every affliction by thinking God's thoughts after Him. When a person violates another person and is brought to true repentance and seeks the forgiveness of the person against whom they have sinned, it may well be the greatest affliction to test the resolve of the abused to do with the sins of another as God has done with theirs.

Like the sore affliction of Job, Satan means to destroy us, but God means to mold us by removing every vestige of self-righteousness and form in us the temperament of the all-forgiving Savior. Like Job, we are made to feel that God "invents pretexts against me; He counts me as His enemy. He puts my feet in the stocks; He watches all my paths" (Job 8:11). But also, like Job, when the Lord has completed His purpose in the sore affliction, we renounce our pre-conceived ideas of what constitutes a genuine spirituality and rise to victory with the resounding note of triumph that God's purposes are being fulfilled in us: "I have heard of You by the hearing of the ear; But now my eye sees You; Therefore I retract, And I repent in dust and ashes" (Job 42:5–6). As contrary as it seems to our humanly conceived ideas, God knows that afflictions that come because of grievous sins committed against us is sometimes the only thing that will work in us the grace and power to forgive as does Christ. "Let all bitterness and wrath and anger and clamor and slander be put away from you, along with all malice. Be kind to one another, tender-hearted, forgiving each other, just as God in Christ also has forgiven you" (Eph 4:31–32). God's all-infinite wisdom knows that only when our commitment to His ways is tested to the limits that we will we push closer to truly "destroying speculations and every lofty thing raised up against the knowledge of God, and we are taking every thought captive to the obedience of Christ" (2 Cor 10:5). For some, God's all wise oversight of their entire life, while never being the author of sin, deigns to allow others to sin against them in ways that defy description, even sexual assault. With the deepest reverence and fear, we must say that the ultimate design of such a test is to allow us, in a very small way, to see more clearly the scope and degree of our sin against Him. When our forgiveness is tested to the limits, it compels us to put into full practice the well-beloved proverb that is quoted so glibly and viewed with such little understanding: "Trust in the LORD with all your heart and do not lean on your own understanding. In all your ways acknowledge Him, and He will make your paths straight" (Prov 3:5–6).

I can't think of a trial that would more put to the test the mandate to trust God's Word and not lean on our own humanly conceived ideas than when a person is sexually assaulted. Revenge, hatred, bitterness, depression, and being totally incapacitated is a small list among the natural instinctive responses to sexual abuse. This is true because the greater the trial the greater becomes our natural tendency to lean to our own understanding. Trusting God and not in ourselves runs against our every natural inclination. This is magnified a hundredfold in cases of sexual abuse. When, however, we think the way Scripture advises us and apply the gospel of forgiveness to others as God has so indiscriminately applied it to us, He brings beauty out of ashes and takes marred masses of humanity and turns them into monuments of His grace. He teaches us the glory of forgiveness!

Saint Bernard of Clairvaux, the medieval reformer and mystic who wrote so affectionately of the love of God and was described as the "honey-tongued doctor," made an astute observation regarding the loss of satanic influence over a person who confesses sin and receives forgiveness: "God removes the sin of the one who makes humble confession, and thereby the devil loses the sovereignty he had gained over the human heart."

Forgiveness of sin is seen by the statement that "God removes the sin," which he hastens to say is dependent on confession of sin. The fascinating observation, however, most revolves around his insinuation that when forgiveness is granted, Satan loses his sovereignty over the very heart of the person forgiven. He suggests that before forgiveness, the devil exercises a kind of uncontested rule over his heart. Reading behind the lines, it is obvious to anyone who has any understanding of the power of sin to bring guilt, shame, and condemnation to the innermost being of man, that it is these things that lose their power over a man when he is completely absolved of his sin by God. He is free indeed! When God forgives a man for a sin he has committed against his Christian neighbor, but the neighbor against whom he sinned refuses to grant full forgiveness, it allows Satan to continue exercising a partial rule that the Lord clearly wills to be broken completely.

There is a clear, case-in-point example of this in the New Testament. The followers of Christ in the city of Corinth at one time harbored a member in the church who had engaged in an incestual relationship (likely with his stepmother) and who, for a time, was completely impenitent. Rather than being immensely grieved, the church was arrogant about it. The advice of the Scriptures in this case was to remove the man from any fellowship with the church: "A man is sleeping with his father's wife. And you are proud! Shouldn't you rather have gone into mourning and have put out of your fellowship the man who has been doing this?" (2 Cor 5:1–2). However, by the time Paul wrote the second letter to this church, God had worked in this man's heart to bring about real sorrow and genuine repentance. Despite this fact, instead of extending to the man the offer of forgiveness commanded by the ethic of the gospel, the church community was apparently ruthlessly severe, inflicting on him pure punishment and refusing to forgive him and restore him to the church. In 2 Cor 2:6–11, the apostle, under the inspiration of the Scripture breathed out by God, expounds on this situation. In the most persuasive terms imaginable, this Scripture emphasizes the absolute necessity and obligation to forgive such a person—

> The punishment inflicted on him by the majority is sufficient. Now instead, you ought to forgive and comfort him, so that he will not be overwhelmed by excessive sorrow. I urge you, therefore, to reaffirm your love for him. Another reason I wrote you was to see if you would stand the test and be obedient in everything. Anyone you forgive, I also forgive. And what I have forgiven—if there was anything to forgive—I have forgiven in the sight of Christ for your sake, in order that Satan might not outwit us. For we are not unaware of his schemes. (2 Cor 2:6–11)

Not only did the form of discipline exercised by the church at Corinth run its God-intended course (the inflicted punishment was sufficient), but the proper response to the now repentant deviant went much further. They were urged, with a passion set aflame by the ethic of the gospel, to forgive, comfort and reaffirm their love to him. Paul makes unambiguously clear the reason—without the forgiveness, comfort, and reaffirmation of love, the person stood to be drowned in an ocean of excessive sorrow. When other believers refuse forgiveness it limits the scope of forgiveness, which is meant to run horizontally as much as it runs vertically. An unwillingness to forgive can hinder the full release of the guilty party who has confessed his sin and should receive human forgiveness as much as he has the divine forgiveness. When forgiveness is with-held from those to whom it should be granted it allows Satan to maintain a mastery over us and outwit us by his wicked schemes.

While God's forgiveness is most essential, and the man-to-man forgiveness on the horizontal level is rather insignificant so long as divine forgiveness is given, when Christians refuse to forgive another believer their transgressions, they become a pawn of Satan advancing an accusatory, but impotent agenda. Why impotent? Because "the accuser of our brethren has been thrown down, he who accuses them before our God day and night" (Rev 12:10). The unforgiving Christian effectively mimics the worst characteristic of Satan, who makes accusations against Christians to God constantly and continually throws in their face sins that God has removed and erased. Any kind of unforgiving, accusatory spirit against a Christian who has confessed his sin and sought forgiveness resists the verdict of forgiveness which God Himself has made to be the last word through the offering of Christ. The unforgiving person acts to ensure that the guilt, shame, and condemnation of the person guilty of the offense will be left "ever before their face." While God has completely forgiven the penitent and cleansed him from all unrighteousness, the non-forgiver insists on an approach that would leave him uncleansed and defiled with a thousand active contaminants.

I know from first-hand experience the urgent need to keep our physical bodies free of chemical contaminants that can ruin our lives and even cause death. My older brother suffered from a kidney disease called hydra-nephrosis (water on the kidney), a disorder experienced in the womb that eventually destroyed his kidneys. Since I was a perfect tissue and blood type, I was the obvious choice to donate him a kidney which was transplanted in 1987 (which, by the way, is still functioning perfectly after thirty-six years, far past the average lifespan of a donated kidney). The kidney, a bean-shaped organ, is about the size of a fist. They are sophisticated reprocessing machines and are critical to cleansing dangerous waste from our systems. Every day, a person's kidneys process about two-hundred quarts of blood to sift out about two quarts of waste products and extra water. After the body has taken what it needs from food, the kidneys function to remove the waste. If the kidneys cease to function correctly, these wastes are left in the blood stream causing severe damage to the overall health of the person. The actual removal of waste occurs in tiny units inside the kidneys called nephrons. Each kidney has about a million nephrons and in the nephron is the glomerulus. The glomerulus acts as a filter and keeps normal proteins and cells in the bloodstream, allowing extra fluid and waste to pass through. A complicated chemical exchange takes place, as waste materials and water leave the blood.

At a doctor's appointment some years ago, due to severe lower back problems, my physician became quite upset with me because, to prevent inflammation in my back muscles, I was taking unusually high doses of ibuprofen that he said would scar the one kidney I have left. The physical importance of our contaminant-cleansing organ cannot be overstated. The regular removal of junk from our physical system has a direct bearing on how we feel daily. During the time before my brother's transplant and the complete malfunction of his kidneys, he would become deathly sick, and it was very hard to watch him suffer this way. Before the transplant, his condition became so serious that he had to have his blood artificially filtered several times a week through dialysis. We thank God for the availability of such life-saving technology, but it can't come close to cleansing us the way God designed through the proper function of the kidneys. In addition, living on dialysis is no way to live long term; ask anyone who has been on dialysis.

It is no hyperbole that the function of our waste removing organs are comparable to the spiritual provision that God has ordained to continually keep our souls free of contaminating sins. The provision He has ordained is the forgiveness of sins made possible, objectively by the death of Christ and obtained subjectively by admission and confession of our sins. If the work of confession and forgiveness cease to function in the way God ordained, there is a build-up of things destructive to our souls. Therefore, the old adage, "keep a short account of your sins," is essential. The constant removal of sin is vital to a healthy conscience. One indication that the full effect of God's forgiveness is not effectually working in our lives to the extent that it should is when forgiveness is granted vertically from God to the sinner, but does not effectually work because, on the horizontal level, a person refuses to forgive a penitent who has confessed his sin and asked for forgiveness. In a sense, it's like being on spiritual dialysis. Yes, the blood is being cleansed, but it is far from being as effectual as it should because the unforgiving person won't grant the same extent of forgiveness as does God, which is free and absolute! When this happens, the sins of a penitent person that are admitted and confessed have a greater potential to fester in the memory, precisely because only one half of the persons who should grant forgiveness (God and fellow man) have done so. In the same way a diseased kidney has a limited ability to effectively remove waste from our physical being, an unwillingness to freely forgive another person of their sin leaves a blemish and scar on the memory of the person from whom it should be removed.

It may be that the worst aspect of the psychology of control is that it can potentially deteriorate into behavioral conduct that actively repudiates the ethic of the gospel. Rather than forgiving and erasing the sin, after the model of what Christ does with our sins, the controller will repeat seventy times seven the sins of another rather than forgiving seventy times seven. When confession of sin is made, unless there are obvious indications of insincerity evident to numerous discerning Christians, there is absolutely no legitimacy whatsoever to withholding full and complete forgiveness. Imagining that you can judge the motives of a Christian making confession of their sin and supposing that your deeper insights qualify you to judge what only God can see is tenuous at best and soul endangering at worst.

> For if you forgive others for their transgressions, your heavenly Father will also forgive you. But if you do not forgive others, then your Father will not forgive your transgressions. . . . And his lord, moved with anger, handed him over to the torturers until he should repay all that was

owed him. My heavenly Father will also do the same to you, if each of you does not forgive his brother from your heart (Matt 6:14–15; 18:34–35).

In the end, all forgiveness, based on the model of Christ's forgiveness of our sins after the ethic of the gospel always works toward reconciled relationships.

Brethren, even if anyone is caught in any trespass, you who are spiritual, restore such a one in a spirit of gentleness; each one looking to yourself, so that you too will not be tempted. Bear one another's burdens, and thereby fulfill the law of Christ. For if anyone thinks he is something when he is nothing, he deceives himself (Gal 6:1–3).

As a caveat to this, because cases of sexual abuse are outside of the realm of what we might call the more normative expressions of sin but involve sins that reveal the perpetrator acted in a way profoundly and abnormally twisted in the extreme, the consequences may never allow for the complete restoration and normalization of the relationship in this life. Nevertheless, when every indicator points to genuine repentance on the part of the perpetrator and their willingness to endure the just punishment for their sinful crime, forgiveness should be extended as freely to them as God's forgiveness has been freely extended to us. Again, there is no legitimacy whatsoever to refusing forgiveness to another sinner who has confessed his sin and sought forgiveness (Matt 18:21–35; Eph 4:32; Col 2:13). Brauns writes, "Forgiveness is a commitment by the offended to pardon graciously the repentant from moral liability and to be reconciled to that person, although not all consequences are necessarily eliminated."[25]

Grace: Is it Fair?

I recently attended the funeral of the wife of a dear friend and colleague in ministry. Her name was Grace, and it was a fitting name because it was clear to all who knew her testimony that she was a living example of this preeminent Christian principle. Her husband preached the sermon for her memorial service. I will never forget a statement he made in the sermon. It is a fitting segue into observing the place of grace as the operative principle in forgiving people of the worst forms of offense. He commented—

> It has been asked, why do bad things happen to good people? Let me say that has only happened one time in history—at the cross.

If you think about it, the underlying point in this funeral sermon statement is a direct, frontal assault on something inherently wrong in the natural thinking system of all people. We all have a very twisted sense of *justice*, of what is fair. To ask why bad things happen to good people is more a statement than a question. The actual statement being made under the guise of

---

[25] Chris Brauns, *Unpacking Forgiveness: Biblical Answers for Complex Questions and Deep Wounds* (Wheaton, IL: Crossway Books, 2008), 55.

the question could be more accurately said this way—"it is unfair when bad things happen to good people. It is a complete miscarriage of justice for good people to have really bad things happen to them. God is unjust!" This is a different question than "why do the righteous suffer?" Frankly, when really bad things happen to people, it is not just Christians who look to God as the ultimate cause. While Christians can struggle with the events God allows into their lives, the right attitude is to see behind terrible events the sovereignty of an infinitely good God. Christians have an implicit trust in God's good character, and we know the design of His will has a good purpose; even when facing catastrophic events which are incomprehensible by any human standard. Unbelievers, however, even though they will often live life with little or no reference to God, also look to God as the sovereign source and cause of events, especially when life deals them the harshest of blows. "The eyes of all look to you" (Ps 145:15). The difference is they don't look to God with implicit trust that He has a good design in what He has allowed. They look to God with an accusatory tone and level at Him the charge of injustice. "How can a good God ever let that happen?"

It may not be readily apparent at this point, but there is a direct correlation between our sense of justice and injustice and the role that a thorough understanding of grace has in our ability and willingness to grant full forgiveness when those who have sinned against us admit, confess, repent, and ask our forgiveness. I have said much about the "genius" of the gospel ethic in forgiving sin. What is essential to understand is that grace is the chief attribute and the indispensable element behind the "genius" of the gospel of forgiveness! Grace is the essential dynamic that enables us to fully forgive after the model of Christ: "bearing with one another, and forgiving each other, whoever has a complaint against anyone; just as the Lord forgave you, so also should you" (Col 3:13). The grace that enables us to forgive others of their transgression so freely is a grace that works "through us" because it first happened "to us." It is being a recipient of grace-based forgiveness that enables us to offer grace-based forgiveness so indiscriminately to others. We all receive from Christ's abundance one gracious gift of forgiveness on top of another: grace for grace, grace stacked on top of grace, grace against grace, grace exchanged for grace, and grace repeated *ad infinitum* (John 1:16). The constancy of our offenses against God necessitates His incessant grace. Such grace is the *modus operandi* behind the forgiveness of our sins. Receiving such a perpetual flow of grace as sinners, we are taught to forgive others in the same spirit of grace. Philip Doddridge eloquently expressed the essence of grace when he penned these words:

> Grace 'tis a charming sound,
> Harmonious to the ear;
> Heaven shall with echo now resound,
> And all the earth shall hear.
> Saved by grace alone!
>
> Grace all thy work shall crown
> Through everlasting days;

It lays in love the topmost stone,
And well deserves the praise.[5]

To grip even more fully the genius of how God's grace works in forgiving us all manner of trespasses against Him and how we forgive all manner of trespasses against us, God's infinite grace must be set alongside of God's infinite justice. It is only when we have a robust understanding of how God's grace intersects with a right view of God's justice that our minds are biblically informed in a way that allows us to forgive as does God, especially when the mandate to forgive is stretched to the limit. It is grace and grace alone that allows us to do with the sins of others as God has done with ours. Applying it even more specifically, the genius of grace must work as effectually through us in forgiving others of their sins as it works effectually through God in forgiving us of our sins: "Whenever you stand praying, forgive, if you have anything against anyone, so that your Father who is in heaven will also forgive you your transgressions" (Mark 11:25). Accurately interpreting the place of grace in its relationship to God's justice is the key to rightly navigating the challenges of extending full and unconditional forgiveness to those who have sinned against us in appalling ways.

In fully exploring the subject of applying the ethic of the gospel of Christ to cases of sexual abuse, particularly as it relates to forgiveness of sin, this section on the relationship between the justice of God and the grace of God is far and away the most

---

[5] Philip Doddridge, "Grace! 'Tis a Charming Sound," 1775.

important consideration in this book. The forthcoming facts are not pedantic but are vital to a more comprehensive understanding of God's grace. Since the message of the Bible is inherently a doctrinal message, that is, it makes clear propositions that those who confess to be Christians must accept and believe, I beg the reader to seriously consider the following doctrinal exposition. It is "the" essential genius when men's capacity to forgive is stretched to extreme limits. All doctrine is meant to be practical, not dry, and irrelevant. If we are to come even close to a practical application of the glory of forgiveness when it is most difficult, it must rest on the foundation of a replete understanding of God's grace. As Charles Haddon Spurgeon said, "Nothing makes a man so virtuous as belief of the truth. A lying doctrine will soon beget a lying practice. A man cannot have an erroneous belief without by-and-by having an erroneous life. I believe the one thing naturally begets the other."[6]

Understanding God's Justice

Generally speaking, the attribute of God's justice is virtually synonymous with the "righteousness" of God. This is evident from the fact that the over eighty uses of the Greek word underlying the concept is virtually always translated by either the word "right," "righteousness," or "just." At the least, the two attributes of justice and righteousness are inseparable because

---

[6] Charles H. Spurgeon, "The Holy Ghost—The Great Teacher," Sermon delivered November 18, 1855. https://www.spurgeon.org/wp-content/uploads/2020/03/The_Holy_Ghost-_The_Great_Teacher.pdf.

behind God's perfect justice in action is His perfect righteousness in character. Justice or righteousness, which is an attribute of God, may be thoroughly defined by noting five elements: 1) God's justice refers to His always being right as opposed to the possibility of ever being wrong in any way. It is perfect correctness. 2) God's justice is eternally constant—He is always just and righteous. 3) God's justice, in the broadest and most general sense, refers to absolute conformity to a perfect standard. The standard is God Himself. In other words, God is the model that exhaustively defines and characterizes righteousness and justice and no other being in the universe is inherently just or righteous. He alone is righteous! 4) God's attribute of justice and righteousness is infinite, immeasurable. What makes God's conformity to the standard so perfect and what makes His model of justice and rightness so infinitely immeasurable is that there is never any deviation in the slightest degree from his justice and righteousness throughout all time and eternity. 5) Finally, God deals with all men completely and strictly in keeping with His justice. Both in His character and in His actions, He deals with men in perfect rectitude (justice and righteousness):

> For I proclaim the name of the LORD; Ascribe greatness to our God! The Rock! His work is perfect, for all His ways are just; A God of faithfulness and without injustice, righteous and upright is He . . . Far be it from You to do such a thing, to slay the righteous with the wicked, so that the righteous and the wicked are treated alike. Far be it from You! Shall

not the Judge of all the earth deal justly? (Deut 32:3–4; Gen 18:25).

As it relates to the doctrine of salvation, which encompasses the grace of God as the genius behind forgiveness of sins, it is impossible for God to ever act contrary to the very essence of His character. For God to act inconsistently with His infinite justice would obliterate any right notion of the person of God. God is incapable of being prejudiced or inequitable. "This God—his way is perfect; the word of the LORD proves true" (2 Sam 22:31). From that foundation of a right understanding of God's justice and righteousness, it is critical to note that God's infinitely perfect justice has three implications for all mankind. Understanding these implications is foundational to understanding the grace of God in man's salvation and forgiveness:

1) Holy Scripture has rendered a clear and unequivocal verdict of guilt over all mankind. "Now we know that whatever the Law says, it speaks to those who are under the Law, so that every mouth may be closed and all the world may become accountable to God" (Rom 3:19).

The word translated "accountable" comes from the same word as do the words just and righteous. The single word accountable is literally the word "under-justice" or "under-righteousness." To be literal, we would have to translate the entire expression as follows—"and all the world may become under-justice to God." In context, it means that the entire world of men, as judged by the standard of God's just requirements outlined in His laws, are guilty of breaking them and are therefore "under sentence." As the old King James version says, "that every mouth may be stopped, and all the world may become guilty before God."

2) Holy Scripture emphatically declares that God, based on His infinite justice, can never acquit the guilty. He acts toward men based on pure, raw justice. Such an infinitely just character forbids Him from declaring anyone to be innocent (or righteous) when according to the facts and based on the standard of His perfect Law, they are guilty. Along with the following explicit statements of this truth contained in the Scriptures, any reasonable attempt to objectively interpret the Scripture, as well as basic human reason and logic, would conclude God is incapable of the kind of twisted justice that would declare innocent a person who is clearly guilty.

> The LORD is slow to anger and abundant in lovingkindness, forgiving iniquity and transgression; but He will by no means clear the guilty, visiting the iniquity of the fathers on the children to the third and the fourth generations. . . . If I sin, then You would take note of me, and would not acquit me of my guilt (Num 14:18; Job 10:14).

3) God's infinite righteousness demands the just penalty for man's sinful guilt. Since it is an indisputable fact that the Bible teaches all men are sinful and guilty, then an infinitely just and righteous God is bound by His own infinitely just character to

punish men accordingly. The entire principle for the punishment of sin, whether being executed by God or man, is rooted in a right sense of justice.

> And we know that the judgment of God rightly falls upon those who practice such things. But do you suppose this, O man, when you pass judgment on those who practice such things and do the same yourself, that you will escape the judgment of God? Or do you think lightly of the riches of His kindness and tolerance and patience, not knowing that the kindness of God leads you to repentance? But because of your stubbornness and unrepentant heart you are storing up wrath for yourself in the day of wrath and revelation of the righteous judgment of God, who WILL RENDER TO EACH PERSON ACCORDING TO HIS DEEDS (Rom 2:2–6).

While I have said that sinful man has a twisted sense of justice, you will never meet a person who has no sense of justice whatsoever. In fact, should evidence confirm that a person stole one hundred dollars from a poor man and then, in the court of an unjust judge, the guilty person was given no sentence or requirement to pay back what they had stolen, the poor man would righteously cry out, "that is not fair"; and he would be one hundred percent right. Imagine a child who stole one hundred dollars' worth of vintage baseball cards, was caught red-handed and then punished by having his hand cut off. We all know instinctively that is a miscarriage of justice, as well as an abuse of power, because such a punishment is exceedingly far out of proportion to the nature of the crime. Justice demands that the punishment must fit the crime. Similarly, if a person is proven guilty of the rape and murder of three teenage girls and is sentenced to behavioral counseling and six months of community service, all civilized people would not only cry out for justice but would cry out for blood. And the cry for blood would be a just cry because the only way a just recompense can be made when you in a pre-meditated way shed innocent blood and take the life of another person is to forfeit your own life.

> Whoever sheds man's blood, by man his blood shall be shed, for in the image of God He made man (Gen 9:6).

> Let every person be subject to the governing authorities . . . For rulers are not a terror to good conduct, but to bad. Would you have no fear of the one who is in authority? Then do what is good, and you will receive his approval, for he is God's servant for your good. But if you do wrong, be afraid, for he does not bear the sword in vain. For he is the servant of God, an avenger who carries out God's wrath on the wrongdoer (Rom 13:1, 3–4).

These three implications of God's infinite justice—1) guilt, 2) refusal to ever acquit the guilty, and 3) the demand for a just punishment—together form a classic syllogism. A syllogism is a three-legged logical argument where two stated propositions, if true, make irrefutable a logical conclusion. The syllogism related to the infinite justice of God's character goes like this—

First Proposition – All men are guilty before the all-just God (true).

Second Proposition – The infinitely just God will never acquit guilty men (true).

Conclusion – Therefore, all men must suffer the just penalty for their guilt (the irrefutable conclusion).

This syllogism was proven above by the biblical support given for the two initial propositions as well as the irrefutable conclusion. It is apparent to any person who reads the Bible and interprets its message in a literal way that this is true. All genuine Christians accept this three-legged argument, and it is only an acceptance of these three truths that can properly understand the absolute necessity of Christ's death on the cross in the place of sinners. According to the whole message of Scripture, Jesus Christ was God manifested in the flesh and took on a real human nature[7] to do the following three things: 1) He took on a real human nature to experience every struggle and temptation as do all men.[8] 2) He endured every temptation and solicitation to sin yet lived an impeccably sinless life.[9] Doctrinally speaking, and as it relates to the demands of God's infinite justice, Jesus' sinless life constituted what is called His *active obedience*. His *active obedience* (perfect conformity to God's law) satisfies God's

---

[7] John 1:14; Gal 4:4; Phil 2:5–8; 1 Tim 3:16.

[8] Heb 2:14, 18.

[9] Heb 4:15; 7:26.

just demand for moral perfection and qualifies Jesus to act as a perfect and sinless representative mediator for all men. 3) As a sinless and perfect sacrifice, Jesus took the penalty of sin demanded by God's infinite justice when He died on the cross for sinners. Doctrinally speaking, and as it relates to the demands of God's infinite justice, Jesus' death on the cross constituted what is called His *passive obedience.* His *passive obedience* (willingly dying on the cross in our place) satisfied God's just demand that sin be punished.[10]

The most essential question (really a dilemma), then, as it relates to God's justice, is "how can God justly acquit guilty men?" How can an infinitely just God allow sinful and wholly unrighteous men to share in heaven?[32] How can God provide guilty men with an individual, personal righteousness that His justice requires? In the terminology of Scripture itself, how can God be just and yet justify (declare righteous) guilty sinners?

He does so by executing a two-way legal transaction that fully satisfies the infinite demands of justice. The first aspect of this transaction involves Christ's passive obedience and took place when all the sins of unrighteous, guilty men were charged and imputed to the one righteous, sinless man, Jesus Christ. This legal transaction took place on the cross where the death of Jesus was due to the legal transference of man's sin and guilt on to Him. The imputation of all the guilt and condemnation of man's sin onto the sinless Son of God executed the justice that God's law required for the death of sinners. In that Jesus is God

---

[10] Gen 2:17; Eze 18:4, 20; Rom 6:23.

come in the flesh for the purpose of atoning for man's sin and because He is infinite, He alone could sufficiently pay the penalty for man's sin against an infinitely holy God. By His death, Jesus satisfies God's just demand for the punishment of sin. By His resurrection from the dead, he sealed our justification (Rom 4:25).

The second aspect of this legal transaction takes place whenever an individual guilty sinner admits to his sin, confesses his sin, asks God to forgive him his sin, and places all His faith in Jesus Christ. When the individual sinner places his faith in Christ, all the perfect righteousness of Christ secured in His act of obedience (perfect conformity to all the laws of God) is legally transferred to, imputed to, and credited to the account of the sinner. Just as all the guilt and condemnation of all the sins of mankind were legally imputed and thus charged to Christ on the cross, so all the perfect righteousness of Christ is legally charged and imputed to the sinner when he puts his faith in Him. This was God's eternally ordained way to satisfy His own infinite justice. As a result of receiving by faith Jesus Christ as his Savior, the sinner is declared righteous by the imputation of Christ's righteousness, and his legal standing and positional status in the eyes of God is righteous. He has, by faith in Christ, the righteousness of Christ freely given to him. By the imputation of Christ's righteousness, the sinner is as righteous as God. This is how God can provide justification for guilty sinners in a just way. This is the Great Transaction! This is the glory of the gospel!

God presented Christ as a sacrifice of atonement, through the shedding of his blood—to be received by faith. He did this to demonstrate his righteousness (or justice), because in his forbearance he had left the sins committed beforehand unpunished— he did it to demonstrate his righteousness (or justice) at the present time, so as to be just and the one who justifies those who have faith in Jesus (Rom 3:24–26).[33]

God was in Christ reconciling the world to Himself, not counting their trespasses against them. . . . He [God the Father] made Him [God the Son] who knew no sin to be sin on our behalf, so that we might become the righteousness of God in Him (2 Cor 5:19a, 21).

> Tis done—the great transaction's done;
> I am my Lord's, and He is mine;
> He drew me and I followed on,
> Rejoiced to own the call divine.
>
> Complete in Thee! no work of mine
> May take, dear Lord, the place of Thine;
> Thy blood hath pardon bought for me,
> And I am now complete in Thee.

---

[33] The quotation of Romans 3:23–26 is taken from the New International Version for sake of clarity. Both the wording as well as all the substantial doctrinal elements in this passage are communicated very clearly by the NIV.

> Yea, justified! O blessed thought!
> And sanctified! Salvation wrought!
> Thy blood hath pardon bought for me,
> And glorified, I too, shall be![11]

To begin gripping more fully the relationship between God's justice and God's grace, it is vital to note that of all of God's attributes involved in providing man's salvation (love, mercy, kindness etc.), God's grace is the primary attribute that motivated and compelled Him to execute His justice in the punishment of His own Son. He punished His own Son rather than executing His just requirement by punishing us. Grace is the one indispensable principle by which God elected to satisfy His demand for justice through the imputation of sin to Christ on the cross and the imputation of Christ's righteousness to the sinner who places faith in Christ. God justly justifies sinners by the atoning sacrifice of Christ.

> For all have sinned and fall short of the glory of God, and all are justified freely by his **grace** through the redemption that came by Christ Jesus (Rom 3:23).

Understanding God's Grace

It is my contention, while the vast majority of confessing Christians have a basic understanding of grace in the program of God's salvation, that their understanding exists at an elementary

---
[11] Aaron R. Wolfe, "Complete in Thee, No Work of Mine."

and rudimentary level. The fuller significance and wider implications of grace in God's program of salvation are somewhat rough-hewn and in-descript. Consequently, an effort to unfold a more exhaustive understanding of God's grace in the program of His salvation is essential. It will not only increase the depth of our gratitude, but it will enlighten our understanding of the genius of the gospel as it relates to the place of grace in forgiving others the worst imaginable sins. Lest I sound condescending, let me explain what I mean.

For all Christians, our entry into the school of "salvation by grace" has informed and educated our thinking with a good, but elemental comprehension of grace. The understanding of grace, as learned by every Christian, is simply defined as "unmerited" or "undeserved" favor. As a basic definition, this is not erroneous in any way. In fact, such a definition immediately declares the most distinctive aspect of our faith and sets Christianity apart from all other world religions. We are not saved by good works or conformity to God's law. We are saved by a favor from God that we cannot earn or merit, nor do we deserve such grace.

> For by grace you have been saved through faith; and that not of yourselves, it is the gift of God; not as a result of works, so that no one may boast. . . . But when the kindness of God our Savior and His love for mankind appeared, He saved us, not on the basis of deeds which we have done in righteousness, but according to His mercy, by the washing of regeneration and renewing by the Holy Spirit (Eph 2:8–9; Titus 3:4–5).

Another well-known way of communicating the essence of God's grace is the popular acronym for the word grace: **G**od's **R**iches **A**t **C**hrist's **E**xpense! Indeed, all the wealth of God has been given to men at the expense of Christ. He died the death we deserve and thereby manifested the greatest act of undeserved favor ever. Despite such wonderful and classic definitions, the fuller and more glorious implications of grace have not been urged on us sufficiently because the concept of God's infinite grace has not been exhaustively defined in relationship to God's infinite justice.

When the fuller implications of God's grace begin to expand in our understanding, not only will the Christian confess I am saved by unmerited favor and cannot earn acceptance with God by my works; he will also understand that if God had offered no provision of salvation whatsoever, He would be guilty of no injustice. When measured by raw, infinite justice, if God condemned all humanity with no hope of salvation, He would be guilty of no unfairness! If He left all of us to incur the full and just punishment for our sin in eternal damnation, He would maintain an unsullied righteousness. The infinite justice of God's essential character does not obligate Him to save us. His infinite justice obligates Him to judge us. However, and praise be to God for this, rather than interacting with men based on sheer justice alone, He elected to intervene on behalf of guilty man because of His infinite grace: "so that in the ages to come He might show the surpassing riches of His grace in kindness toward us in Christ Jesus" (Eph 2:7). Understanding salvation "by grace alone" is truly more than recognizing we can't earn it;

it is recognizing, from the standpoint of raw justice, that God has absolutely no moral obligation to offer it. That is what is meant by grace! God's justice could fairly condemn us all, but by His unmerited grace and favor, gloriously manifested to us without measure in Christ, He has saved us! This is exactly the argument Paul uses when he argues that the patriarch, Abraham, was not justified by good works along the lines of what justice would demand, but solely on the basis of faith rooted in grace—

> Now to the one who works, his wage is not credited as a favor, but as what is due [justice]. But to the one who does not work, but believes in Him who justifies the ungodly [by grace], his faith is credited as righteousness (Rom 4:4–5).

Even among Christians, our humanly conceived and fallen understanding of what constitutes real justice and fairness causes men to, at best, minimize the full implications of God's grace. At worst, an inability to rightly understand infinite justice can cause us to torture the concept of grace beyond recognition. When really forced to grapple with a grace of this magnitude and a grace rooted in the eternal purposes of God's election, the natural tendency of man is to argue that it can't be right. The reason they argue against grace defined this way is because they see it as unjust and unfair. Consequently, the apostle Paul is compelled, under the inspiration of the Holy Spirit, to defend the concept of electing grace against charges that it is unfair. While advancing the principle of electing grace rooted in the eternal purposes of God, Paul both raises the specific charge leveled against God's justice and refutes it on the principle of infinite grace.

> What shall we say then? There is no injustice with God, is there? May it never be! . . . In the same way then, there has also come to be at the present time a remnant according to God's gracious choice. But if it is by grace, it is no longer on the basis of works, otherwise grace is no longer grace (Rom 9:14, 11:5–6).

A little home-spun parable may help to elucidate the fuller implications of what we mean by infinite grace when seen in relationship to infinite justice. Imagine that a business owner enters a contract with a cleaner to come and do a one-time comprehensive clean-up of his office building: sweep, do windows, dust, take out the trash, etc. The cleaner gives him a bid of one-thousand dollars. The owner accepts. The cleaner later comes to the office building and does a fantastic job which meets with the owner's great satisfaction. Later, the cleaner comes to the owner to receive the agreed payment for the contracted work. He owes him the one-thousand dollars. If he refuses to pay, an injustice has occurred. However, imagine that the owner comes in to inspect the work that has been done, and because the cleaner performed his work so much better than he had expected, he gives him two-thousand dollars for the job. Technically, that is not grace, but simply an inclination to be extra good to the man. But if the cleaner had never come to fulfill the terms of the contract and did absolutely no cleaning, justice would require that he be paid nothing. He would not receive the agreed upon amount of one thousand dollars and he would not have received an extra amount out of the good pleasure of the owner.

But let's say, after the deal was struck to clean the office for one thousand dollars, the cleaner refused to fulfill the terms of the contract. Imagine a scenario where he is not only unwilling to clean anything, but worse, he goes in and destroys the office. He turns over the tables, pours the trash all over the floor, throws all the files on the floor, crushes all the computers, and destroys all other equipment. Finally, the cleaner dumps a truck load of manure in the middle of the office and hurls it on the walls. Symbolically, this scenario represents God's original probation with man in the garden which He promised blessing on the condition that man justly and legally meet the terms of the divinely given contract. As with Adam in the garden, the cleaner not only fails to fulfill the terms of the contract, but he exacerbates the problem by all the extra mischief for which he is guilty. The reckless cleaner has no sense that the owner is going to do a surprise inspection. He shows up at the office unannounced to see the quality of the job assigned to the cleaner. Not only does he find the room in worse condition than before, but he observes that the cleaner is sitting down and wallowing right in the middle of the mound of manure. The owner then goes over to the cleaner, looks at him with eyes of full of pity, then reaches into his wallet and gives the man a million dollars. That is GRACE.

Ultimately, in synthesizing the elements of God's justice and God's grace, it will help us to re-word the entire statement made by my friend at the funeral of his wife. My friend asked, "Why do bad things happen to good people?" He then answered his own question, "Well, that has happened only one time in history—at the cross." To aid us in more fully comprehending grace, let's ask and answer the question this way: "How can God justly save unrighteous people and give them eternal life? Well, that happens all the time—at salvation." It happens all the time because, in the past, God satisfied His own inherent demand for infinite justice when the eternal Son of God paid the penalty for man's sin on the cross of Calvary. It happens all the time because, in the present, whenever a person places faith in Christ, the crediting and imputation of Christ's perfect righteousness provides the individual believer with the righteousness required for acceptance in God's presence. God is both just and the justifier of him who believes in Jesus!

This understanding of justice alongside of grace provides the genius by which the victim of a sexual assault is enabled to forgive their repentant assailant of such an indescribable sin fully and freely. They can because they have ceased to process issues of sin and transgression purely along the lines of justice alone. The ethic of the gospel of Jesus Christ has taught them to apply something more to transgressors than pure justice. The gospel has taught them that if God interacted with them solely on the basis of justice, He would be obligated to turn them over to the judge, to throw them into the eternal prison, and to not let them out till they had paid up the last cent.[12] The gospel has taught them that their sins against God are infinite because He is an infinite person. The gospel of Christ has taught them that any sin against them, which can admittedly be of the most horrific kind, are miniscule in comparison to their sins against an infinitely holy God. The gospel that causes justice and grace to kiss each other has taught them that it is a pure joy to forgive others of so little when they have been forgiven so much! The gospel has taught them the glory of forgiveness. The gospel has taught them to forgive others as God forgives them.

> Lovingkindness and truth have met together; Righteousness and peace have kissed each other (Ps 85:10).

> For this reason I say to you, her sins, which are many, have been forgiven, for she loved much; but he who is forgiven little, loves little (Luke 7:47).

> For this reason the kingdom of heaven may be compared to a king who wished to settle accounts with his slaves. When he had begun to settle them, one who owed him ten thousand talents was brought to him. But since he did not have the means to repay, his lord commanded him to be sold, along with his wife and children and all that he had, and repayment to be made. So the slave fell to the ground and prostrated himself before him, saying, "Have patience with me and I will repay you everything." And the lord of

---

12 Matt 5:25–26.

that slave felt compassion and released him and forgave him the debt (Matt 18:23–27).

Victimization: The Ultimate Sufferer and the Scapegoat

Comparisons are a part of life. We draw comparisons between different things all the time. Comparisons serve us well. We mark the height of our child on a tape-measure-line drawn on the back of their bedroom door when they are five-years old and compare it with a mark that measured their height at one-year old. Charting growth allows our children to have a tangible sense of progress. Sometimes, however, comparisons do not serve us well. They can be absolutely the worst way to make a point—like trying to compel a teenager struggling to master algebra to do better by drawing a negative comparison between him and a child in his class who is a math whiz: "Your friend Johnny has no problem with algebra; why can't you do it like him?" Making unflattering spiritual comparisons between one Christian and another is always a source of division and is highly discouraged in Scripture, "for we are not bold to class or compare ourselves with some of those who commend themselves; but when they measure themselves by themselves and compare themselves with themselves, they are without understanding" (2 Cor 10:12).

However, when taking a decidedly scriptural approach to the question of forgiving others of the most despicable sins against us, comparison is essential. Specifically, part of the genius to forgiving others of the worst imaginable sins against us demands a comparison between the guilt of our personal sin against God on the vertical level set next to the guilt of any sin committed against us on the horizontal level. This becomes a most delicate matter in cases of sexual abuse. However, such a comparison is not only advocated and exemplified in Scripture but doing so in a proper way exposes the genius of the gospel of forgiveness in the most spiritually astute way possible. This is exactly what Jesus does in the parable of the king who settled accounts (Matt 18:23–35). In this masterful lesson on the forgiveness of sins, there is an inspired comparison drawn between a slave who was forgiven an enormous amount of debt by his master and then, rather than forgiving a fellow slave who owed him a mere pittance, absolutely refused to forgive him. The forgiven slave, whose master forgave his entire debt on the principle of compassionate grace, then went out and exacted the full amount of his debtor based on raw justice. The irony of the story is apparent, and the parable drives home the main gospel lesson in unmistakable fashion. Our sins against an infinitely holy God are exorbitant in comparison to the meager sins committed against us by others. We are every bit as sinfully depraved as others, though our sins may not find expression in the same extreme way. Therefore, having been forgiven a debt of sin far greater than we will ever have to forgive, Jesus' mandate to forgive is urged on us with an appropriately excessive force.

It is hard to express to another person how any victim of sexual abuse arises to this level of grace, magnanimity, and forgiveness. It is unquestionably a divinely omnipotent work of the Holy Spirit impressed on the person through the message of

Scripture. The Holy Spirit uses different circumstances to teach us the importance of unconditionally forgiving others as God does us. The principal truth that works this forgiving grace in our life, however, is when we realize, because of a conscious awareness of the depth of our own sin and depravity, that the gap between any sin committed against us set next to our sins against God is infinitely disproportionate. If there was a literal spiritual measuring stick that could accurately compare the sins that others have committed against us compared to the sins we commit against God, it would be the difference between a millimeter set next to a trillion galaxies stacked on top of each other. It would be the difference between a Planck Length (the smallest possible size for anything in the universe) set next to a googol (the largest number we have—10^{100}, or ten multiplied by itself 100 times, or a 1 with 100 zeroes behind it). In fact, since God is spiritually infinite in His holiness (limitless and immeasurable), and since we are so sinfully finite in our willful depravity, there is no possible way to compare our sins against God to the sins that other finite beings have committed against us. The gulf is infinitely wide. There is simply no comparison!

It is truly an other-earthly thing, a deeply spiritual and divine accomplishment, for a person to become so acutely aware of the magnitude of their own sin against God that they view terrible sins committed against them as microscopic by comparison. It is a heaven-given ability that can only be experienced by a genuine Christian because only Christians are taught to forgive in accordance with the ethic of the gospel of forgiveness. The ethic of the gospel, that the all-infinite Son of

God took on Himself the enormity of our sins against Him, informs the mind of the forgiven Christian, gripped by faith alone, that our sins against Him infinitely outweigh any sin our fellow man has sinned against us. The sins that others have committed against us is but a drop in a bucket compared to the Pacific volume of sins we have committed against God. It is this level of gospel genius that can rightly mandate that we freely and fully forgive others, no matter their crimes against us. It is this gospel truth that can then condition God's forgiveness of us on our willingness to forgive others.

> And Jesus answered saying to them, "Have faith in God. Truly I say to you, whoever says to this mountain, 'Be taken up and cast into the sea,' and does not doubt in his heart, but believes that what he says is going to happen, it will be granted him. Therefore I say to you, all things for which you pray and ask, believe that you have received them, and they will be granted you. Whenever you stand praying, forgive, if you have anything against anyone, so that your Father who is in heaven will also forgive you your transgressions. But if you do not forgive, neither will your Father who is in heaven forgive your transgressions" (Mark 11:22–26).

> What love could remember no wrongs we have done
> Omniscient, all knowing, he counts not their sum
> Thrown into a sea without bottom or shore
> Our sins they are many, his mercy is more.

> What patience would wait as we constantly roam
> What father, so tender, is calling us home
> He welcomes the weakest, the vilest, the poor
> Our sins they are many, his mercy is more.
>
> What riches of kindness he lavished on us
> His blood was the payment, his life was the cost
> We stood 'neath a debt we could never afford
> Our sins they are many, his mercy is more.[13]

If I might add a line to this song in keeping with the immensity of our sin committed against God next to the incomparably insignificant sins committed against us, it would go like this—

> What sins could compare with the sin against God
> Great in enormity, exceedingly broad
> No sin against others, whatever the crime
> Could ever compare with forgiveness Divine.

It is immensely sad that some people have been victimized at the sinful hands of others. But you must know, without question, that others have been victimized by your sinful hands. Yes, by comparison to the sins of others, your crimes may fall into what we would regard as a "lesser offense." Before an

---

[13] Matt Papa and Matt Boswell, "His Mercy Is More," *Church Songs*, 2016.

THE GLORY OF FORGIVENESS

infinitely holy God, however, there is no lesser offense. Every mouth is stopped, and we are all guilty before God.[14] To say it as bluntly and straightforward as possible, you have victimized God far more than you have ever been victimized by another. This is true of all of us. When we begin to get close to the glory of forgiveness extended to exceedingly sinful sinners such as us, this truth is accepted without reservation. Jesus Christ, the lamb of God that takes away the sins of the world[15] is the ultimate victim. "For even Christ did not please Himself; but as it is written, "THE REPROACHES OF THOSE WHO REPROACHED YOU FELL ON ME'" (Rom 15:3). He has been victimized at the guilty hands of sinners. He is victimized by all of us. The glory of forgiveness is the glad assurance that He has forgiven and removed our colossal sins against Him. The glory of forgiveness, following His infinitely perfect model, is to forgive others.

Such a comment—that you have victimized God far more than you have ever been victimized—is made with the deepest respect for girls and boys and women and men who have suffered so cruelly by the incalculable selfishness of a sexual abuser. These comments are made with the most guarded and profound sense that they accurately reflect the truth and communicate the will of God's own heart. Yet, they are made dogmatically because they do! "For Christ also died for sins once for all, the just for the unjust" (1 Pet 3:18). If anyone other than Christ could claim a

---

[14] Rom 3:19.

[15] John 1:29.

perfectly just status, then they might have a claim that their victimization is near to that of Christ. Since, however, we all fall into the category of the unjust, no such claim can be made. It is the full comprehension of this truth, made by comparison, that sets the prisoner of sexual assault free. It sets them free because, having been forgiven for the enormity of all their unjust deeds against an infinitely just Savior, they are enabled by the ethic of the gospel to forgive a fellow unjust sinner of their sins against them.

There is not a more beautiful picture of Christ being victimized and the victimizer being set free than in the live goat and scapegoat sacrifice made on the Jewish Day of Atonement. This divinely prescribed ceremony was clearly an Old Testament, symbolic foreshadowing of what Christ would do in paying the price for our sin, thus providing the basis for the complete forgiveness and removal of our sins.

> He shall take from the congregation of the sons of Israel two male goats for a sin offering. . . . He shall take the two goats and present them before the LORD at the doorway of the tent of meeting. Aaron shall cast lots for the two goats, one lot for the LORD and the other lot for the scapegoat. Then Aaron shall offer the goat on which the lot for the LORD fell and make it a sin offering. But the goat on which the lot for the scapegoat fell shall be presented alive before the LORD, to make atonement upon it, to send it into the wilderness as the scapegoat. . . . Then Aaron shall lay both of his hands on the head of the live goat, and confess over it

all the iniquities of the sons of Israel and all their transgressions in regard to all their sins; and he shall lay them on the head of the goat and send it away into the wilderness by the hand of a man who stands in readiness. The goat shall bear on itself all their iniquities to a solitary land; and he shall release the goat in the wilderness (Lev 16:5–10, 21–22).

By prescribing two male goats be part of the sacrifice, the Lord was painting a graphic picture of 1) the essential necessity that a life be taken to bear the sins of others in a substitutionary sacrifice, and 2) that the sins of others would be forgiven and removed. The male goat to be sacrificed and the male goat to be set free (scapegoat) were determined by the casting of lots. The casting of lots was an Old Testament provision for determining the will and choice of God. The fact that the fate of the slain goat as well as the scapegoat were determined by the casting of lots indicated the choice was completely under the sovereignty of God. It was a picture that Jesus would be delivered over by the predetermined plan and foreknowledge of God.[16] The real beauty and timeless lesson is that the slaughtered goat pictured the necessity that Jesus bear in His body the consequence for our sins. The freeing of the scapegoat pictured that our sins were carried far away, into an unknown and uncharted area like to the wilderness where the scapegoat was banished. It is a picture of our cleansing by forgiveness. As noted by Matthew Henry, "one

---

[16] Acts 2:23.

of these goats must be slain, in token of a satisfaction to be made to God's justice for sin, the other must be sent away, in token of the remission or dismission of sin by the mercy of God."[17] As Albert Barnes commented—

> It is evident that the one signification of the ceremony of this goat was the complete removal of the sins which were confessed over him. No symbol could so plainly set forth the completeness of Yahweh's acceptance of the penitent, as a sin-offering in which a life was given up for the altar, and yet a living being survived to carry away all sin and uncleanness.[18]

The placing of the hands of the priest on the scapegoat, over which was made confession for all the iniquities of God's people and regarding all of their sins, foreshadowed the transference of all the accomplishments of Christ for His people. Like the scapegoat, our sins are now in the vast wilderness of God's forgetfulness and have been placed in their totality beyond the recall of His memory. "Gone, gone, gone, gone; yes, my sins are gone! Buried in the deepest sea, into the Sea of Forgetfulness. Never to be remembered anymore." Indeed, our sins are removed "as far as the east is from the west, so far has He removed our transgressions from us" (Ps 103:12).

---

[17] Matthew Henry, "Leviticus 16," *Matthew Henry Bible Commentary.*

[18] Albert Barnes, ed., "Leviticus 16," *Barnes' Notes on the Whole Bible,* Accessed July 20, 2023.
https://www.studylight.org/commentaries/eng/bnb/leviticus.html.

THE GLORY OF FORGIVENESS

The apostle Paul, a man who wrote thirteen of the twenty-seven New Testament letters and whose influence God determined would spread the gospel ethic to the whole known world, once referred to himself as the "chief of sinners."[19] While the confession primarily expresses the idea that he was set forth by God's design as a model and prototype of God's salvation by grace and apart from works, there is no way, as he made this confession, that he would not have thought about the terrible litany of sins he committed against God and against others. Before he came to Christ and before being forgiven of his sins, among other things, he was guilty of blasphemy, evil, spearheading the unjust incarceration of women and men, and violent aggression; he was furiously enraged by anger and guilty of murder. So oppressive was the memory of what he had done that, after his conversion, he testified that "I am the least of the apostles, and not fit to be called an apostle, because I persecuted the church of God" (1 Cor 15:9). Despite his colossal guilt, not only did God forgive and remove his sin, but the entire early church embraced him as a rare object of God's saving grace. Having been guilty of their own sins by the genius of a gospel that knows no limits of forgiveness, they freely forgave him. Coming to embrace the glory of forgiveness and then extending it to others is not a mere piece of theological claptrap. The glory of forgiveness has a practical power and impact on life that is singularly the most distinguishing and unique element of gospel-driven relationships.

---

[19] 1 Tim 1:15.

Such forgiveness, when rooted in an understanding that infinite justice demanded that the full extent of God's wrath fall on Christ to forgive sin, does not cheapen grace. Neither does it make the forgiveness of all sin automatic by virtue of Christ's death. If that were the case, the false doctrine of Universalism would go uncontested. Forgiveness is conditioned on a biblical recognition of the enormity of our sinful guilt as well as genuine repentance (not mere emotional sorrow for wrongdoing). When these elements are worked into the heart by the operation of the Holy Spirit, the forgiveness offered by God through Christ becomes forgiveness applied through Christ. As it is on the divine-to-human level, so must it be on the human-to-human level. This wonderful scriptural balance obliterates the cheap, no-repentance-required forgiveness so dominant in the thinking of many people. In recent times, the testimony of Rachael Denhollander, one of the many victims of sexual abuse at the hands of Larry Nassar, is most insightful and hopeful. She addressed her abuser in the following terms—

> In our early hearings. you brought your Bible into the courtroom, and you have spoken of praying for forgiveness. And so it is on that basis that I appeal to you. If you have read the Bible you carry, you know the definition of sacrificial love portrayed is of God himself loving so sacrificially that he gave up everything to pay a penalty for the sin he did not commit. By his grace, I, too, choose to love this way.

You spoke of praying for forgiveness. But Larry, if you have read the Bible you carry, you know forgiveness does not come from doing good things, as if good deeds can erase what you have done. It comes from repentance which requires facing and acknowledging the truth about what you have done in all of its utter depravity and horror without mitigation, without excuse, without acting as if good deeds can erase what you have seen this courtroom today. If the Bible you carry says it is better for a stone to be thrown around your neck and you throw into a lake than for you to make even one child stumble. And you have damaged hundreds. The Bible you speak carries a final judgment where all of God's wrath and eternal terror is poured out on men like you. Should you ever reach the point of truly facing what you have done, the guilt will be crushing. And that is what makes the gospel of Christ so sweet. Because it extends grace and hope and mercy where none should be found. And it will be there for you. I pray you experience the soul crushing weight of guilt so you may someday experience true repentance and true forgiveness from God, which you need far more than forgiveness from me— though I extend that to you as well. Throughout this process, I have clung to a quote by C.S. Lewis, where he says, my argument against God was that the universe seems so cruel and unjust. But how did I get this idea of just, unjust? A man does not call a line crooked unless he first has some idea of straight. What was I comparing the universe to when I called it unjust?[20]

As soul staggering as it is and as far from the false, humanly conceived notions of forgiveness we all have, the words of Rachael Denhollander, spoken to her terrible abuser, can be justly leveled at every sinner who has abused the all-innocent lamb of God. We too must recognize we need a "repentance which requires facing and acknowledging the truth about what [we] have done in all of its utter depravity and horror without mitigation, without excuse." We all must admit that the Bible "carries a final judgment where all of God's wrath and eternal terror is poured out on men like" us. The final commentary of Jesus on the glory of forgiveness is that the sin of any human against another human, no matter how morally degenerate and murderous, is microscopic in comparison to our sins in the presence of an infinitely just and holy God. The test of whether God has forgiven you the immensity of your sins against Him is whether you will freely, from the heart, forgive men the exceedingly small, infinitesimal sins they have sinned against you.

Points of Practical Pastoral Wisdom	
Primary Goal	In the fourth stage of applying the ethic of the gospel to cases of sexual abuse, the pastor-counselor

---

[20] "Read Rachael Denhollander's Full Victim Impact Statement about Larry Nassar," CNN, January 30, 2018, https://www.cnn.com/2018/01/24/us/rachael-denhollander-full-statement/index.html.

	must showcase forgiveness and teach the counselee to accept and rejoice in the astounding provisions made for sin by the death of Christ.
Real Life Examples	In 2015 Frank Luntz asked Donald Trump whether he has ever asked God for forgiveness for his actions. Trump responded: "I am not sure I have. I just go on and try to do a better job from there. I don't think so," he said. "I think if I do something wrong, I think, I just try and make it right. I don't bring God into that picture. I don't." This is an approach to sin that denies it or tries to atone for it by improvement and good works.
Vital Questions	What is forgiveness of sin/s? How would you define or explain it? Do you believe and are you assured God has forgiven you of all your sins? Do you believe you can withhold forgiveness from a human who has sinned against you and receive forgiveness from God against whom you have sinned? Have you ever struggled or do you now struggle to forgive another person of their sin? Why?
Typical Counselee Responses	Because of guilt associated with their own sins, people struggle to believe that God can and is willing to forgive all their sins freely and fully. There is little doubt a minister has not encountered this in his experience. It becomes a marvelous platform from which to preach the gospel and assure forgiveness through the provision made by Jesus. There is also, on the part of people who have been sinned against in the most egregious ways, a

	tendency to struggle with or refuse altogether to forgive their offender.
Specific Applications	Sin's power, energized by Satan, the accuser of the brothers, tends to leave a scarred imprint on the memory of man. No moral therapeutic determinism can wash away the stain. We are all debtors to God's grace and forgiving mercy; but we are not debtors to His justice, for He will never accuse me of a debt already paid. Christ said, "It is finished!" And by that He meant that whatever His people owed was WIPED AWAY FOR EVER FROM THE BOOK OF REMEMBRANCE. "Forgiveness isn't about forgetting. It is the ability to remember without feeling the emotional sting."
Homework	While there are many passages to assign a person struggling with forgiveness, there are two that we consider as prime texts. For the person struggling to believe God can forgive the enormity of their sin, Psalm 51:1 is gigantic. "Be gracious to me, O God, according to Your lovingkindness; According to the greatness of Your compassion blot out my transgressions." Specifically, ask the counselee to explain the relationship that exists between, "graciousness," "lovingkindness," "compassion," and the blotting out of sin. For the person struggling to forgive another person, ask them to pour over "The Parable of the Unforgiving Servant" in Matthew 18:21–35. Ask them if they understand the point of the financial illustration/comparison and its significance to

| | receiving forgiveness of our own sin. We should not hedge on what is taught here in any way, while allowing time for God to help the person to see the significance and application of the parable. |

CHAPTER 6

The Critical Need for CONTAINMENT: Insulating Others Against Unnecessary Contamination

"He who conceals a transgression seeks love,
But he who repeats a matter separates intimate friend."
(Prov 17:9)

Broad or Narrow: The Circle of People Brought into the Loop

When disclosure, justice, confession, and forgiveness of sin are executed according to the ethic of the gospel in cases of sexual abuse, a vital question remains. It must be asked and answered with a dogged determination to be rigidly true and wise in rightly applying the Holy Scriptures. Here is the question: When a sexual abuser makes a full admission of their guilt and gives every indication of true repentance, how broad should the circle of people be who must be notified about the specifics of the sin?

Should some of the standard axioms typically applied in cases of sin be used without discrimination?

"The circle of people that need to be notified is the circle of people directly affected by the sin."

"Keep the circle of people involved in a conflict as small as possible for as long as possible."

The legal requirements of notification, discussed above under the heading of justice, clearly outline a required set of notifications about which we have no discretion. The circle of people that is required by the law must be notified, no questions asked! A further question, however, is whether the legal circle as well as others who are directly involved in the abuse is wide enough? Once the legal authorities are brought into the circle, along with pastors, psychologists, medical personnel, and parents, should the circle of people be broadened even further? The answer to that question is an emphatic yes! But it is a "yes" which must be implemented with great discernment, tact, and wisdom.

If a Christian is guilty of committing a sin against God alone, in the secret place of his heart that only God sees, notification of the sin through confession need go no further than God. If a Christian is guilty of committing a sin against another person by screaming at them out of control, then notification by confession must move on both a vertical level as well as horizontal level. He has sinned against both God and man. If a Christian man with adult children commits adultery against his wife and she is the only one who knows about it, the notification must go further than her. His sin is not only against God on the vertical level and against his wife on the horizontal level, but the circle of people affected by his violation extends to his family. If he is a member of a Christian church, his sin has affected more people still. He has not only sinned against God, his wife, and his family, but he has also brought public shame on the name of Christ by violating his covenant to live in a way that is in harmony with a confession to be a Christian. The extent of notifications, for the sake of the purity of the church, must be extended even further.

In each case the circle of people notified spreads out no further than the circle of people either directly or indirectly affected by the sin. The sin, as awful as it may be, is contained as far as is possible. The broader and general principle is that the people given knowledge of a sin is the concentric circle of people who, in some way, stand to be impacted by the shockwave of the sin. If a severe thunderstorm stands to affect a two-mile radius from the center of the storm and no further, then those located three miles away need no warning to alert them of the need for shelter. In cases of sexual abuse and molestation, determining how far it stands to affect other people is rather unpredictable. The inexplicable nature of the sin, the degree of the perversity involved, and the extent to which it can be entrenched in the person given to such wickedness makes it nearly impossible to anticipate exactly how far out from ground zero this particular shock wave may be felt. Consequently, extra measures, beyond what is normally practiced in cases of sin must be implemented.

Since helping victims of sexual abuse to heal is such a tenuous and delicate process, every ounce of prevention becomes the mandate determining those who must be notified. Such notification, in the interest of prevention, necessitates the following considerations: Protection, Accountability, Probation, and Consequences.

PROTECTION:
The Primary Consideration for Containment

First, among all other considerations in determining the extent of those who must be notified in cases of sexual abuse is the *protection of the abused person*. All persons who have any familial guardianship responsibilities of a minor who has been abused must be notified. This level of notification is to ensure the child never again stands the risk of such a violation against the sacredness of their person. To provide the highest level of protection against a repeated offense, any person responsible in any way for the care of the child must be alerted about those who pose a risk. They must be given the specific name/s of those who have committed such sinful crimes and they must know the extent to which they have violated others. Even persons who are sexually abused past the time of being a legal adult must be protected against further abuse. They may still be at risk and, therefore, any level of notification necessary to ensure their protection is justified. Assessing ongoing risk is dependent on many factors. Some sexual abusers are guilty of violations way into adulthood and, even when seeking help, may struggle with

THE CRITICAL NEED FOR CONTAINMENT

such urges for the entirety of their lives. Some may have committed a one-time juvenile act of abuse while a minor and have never repeated it nor continue to struggle with it in any way. Whatever the case, the guiding principle is the ongoing protection of the abused.

Secondly, the *protection of others* is paramount in determining the circle of people who must be notified. On the civil level, this is exactly why local and national sources provide a registry of sexual predators. "The Dru Sjodin National Sex Offender Public Website (NSOPW)" is an unprecedented public safety resource that provides the public with access to sex offender data nationwide."[1] Under the acronym, SMART, this organization exists to: Sentence, Monitor, Apprehend, Register, and Track sexual offenders. Why? Yes, to ensure that such crimes are justly punished. But equally important they exist to protect others against such life-altering abuse. Within individual families, when abuse takes place at the hands of a person otherwise thought to be trustworthy, the rule for how broadly to notify others within the larger, extended family should consider several things: 1) Those parents who have minor children must be notified of a family member who poses a continuing risk to the well-being of their child. This is the only way to put them on notice of the potential risk and to provide the necessary protection. 2) In cases where there is virtually no likelihood that another family member's child is at risk and will likely never be in the presence

---

[1] "About NSOPW," Dro Sjodin National Sex Offender Public Website, accessed July 19, 2023. https://www.nsopw.gov/About.

of the sexual abuser, discretion will need to guide the extent to which they need to be notified. This is especially important when a person's sexual sin is comparably moderate and they have repented, been forgiven, and proven themselves by years of blamelessness. The rule is containment, but never at the risk of another child.

Thirdly, the *protection of the testimony of the church* must be taken into consideration. When a church is notified about a case of sexual abuse that took place outside of the jurisdiction of the church or is made aware that a person has violated another person within the church family or on the church premises, decisive action must be immediately taken to make all proper notifications. The foremost consideration motivating such action is the protection of the abused and any others who could be injured by further indecision or negligence on the part of the church. Equally important is that the church, by the proper set of actions and notifications, protect the reputation of Christ Himself. Since churches confessing the Christian faith represent the person of Christ and His teachings, it is vitally important that the church demonstrate that such wickedness is utterly out of step with biblical Christianity. When the right actions are not taken, Christians make themselves liable to charges of tolerating immorality and gross hypocrisy.

In every case where a person of adult age who has committed themselves to the church by way of official membership is proven guilty of sexual abuse, the circle of people notified must encompass the entire church family. All other Christians officially committed to the church by way of

THE CRITICAL NEED FOR CONTAINMENT

membership have the right to know. Such a process for church discipline is mandated by Scripture. It may be helpful to recognize, along with gross sexual immorality, there are five other general categories of sin that must be handled as matters requiring some level of church discipline and require notification of the entire church family: false teaching, heresy, gross deceit, intentionally promoting division, and slanderous defamation of another person's character.[2]

In cases where the leadership of the church is made aware of a more casual attender who is guilty of past acts of sexual abuse, legal matters limit the extent to which they can broadly extend the circle of notifications. To go beyond what is permissible under the law can expose the church to litigation that can be potentially devastating. However, since the protection of others is foremost, the entire leadership team should be notified of the presence of such a person. Furthermore, if a past abuser is serious about getting the help offered through the gospel of Christ and the ethic of biblical Christianity, they will gladly submit to severely limiting guidelines imposed by the leadership of the church. Such limitations should categorically and forever deny the person any right to serve in any kind of children or teen ministry. The restrictions should also involve close monitoring that refuses to allow a past abuser to ever be alone with a child or teen. Should a past abuser violate the protocols established by the leadership of the church, their permission to attend services should be immediately revoked.

---

[2] Matt 18:15–17; 1 Cor 5:1–7; Gal 6:1–4; 1 Thess 5:12–14; Heb 13:7, 17.

ACCOUNTABILITY:
An Essential Feature in Protective Containment

When a church carries out the proper set of notifications, those actions alone are a good starting point and a critical step in applying the need for strict, personal accountability. However, notification alone is not sufficient. A biblical and well-structured accountability must be implemented. Before specifically applying the biblical principles of accountability to the case of a repentant abuser, it will help to establish the general biblical teaching about personal accountability. The biblical teaching regarding personal accountability reveals a vital need of which all Christians should be aware. A few examples will reveal its ultimate purpose and why it is so essential to hold and measure people by the standards for which they will be held accountable. Generally speaking, three broad biblical principles of accountability are revealed: 1) Accountability is universal. All men are held accountable for the way they live their lives.[3] 2) Church leaders are held to a particularly high set of standards and the church is both obligated and vested with the authority to hold them accountable to meeting these standards in an exemplary way.[4] 3) The members of the body of Christ are accountable to one another in the areas of confession, prayer, love, exhortation, forgiveness, service, submission, edification, and comfort.[5]

---

[3] Eccl 12:14; Rom 1:32; 2:3, 16.

[4] 1 Tim 3:1–13; Titus 1:5–9; Jas 3:1.

[5] Jas 5:16; 1 John 4:7; Heb 3:13; Eph 4:32; Col 3:13; Gal 5:13; 1 Pet 4:9;

In each case, the reason for the established measures of accountability is meant to impress on our minds numerous things: 1) The specific moral and spiritual standards to which we will be held accountable are established by divine authority. 2) A just set of consequences will be meted out if the standard is violated. 3) The standards have a power to compel behavior because the known punishment for violating the standards is no empty threat. The work of God's grace and faith in the life of the Christian are critical to our conformity to expected standards, but accountability is a necessary device within the ethic of the gospel. It is among the devices chosen by God to encourage godly conduct.

Applying the general principles of accountability to the specific needs of a sexual abuser demands measures that go far beyond the normal operating principles of accountability. In general, trust is gained when a person's conduct consistently conforms to the lines of behavior along which they are held accountable. Since "trust" is such an essential component in healthy relationships and since the degree of sacred trust is violated so profoundly in cases of sexual abuse, the structures of accountability placed on those guilty of this sin must be especially rigid. Like other sins that cause a permanent loss of trust, or create a great struggle to regain trust, sexual abuse has the power to obliterate trust like nothing else. For this reason, to protect others from abusers and to restrain abusers from further acts of sin, the church must thoughtfully implement a very

---

Heb 10:24; Eph 5:21; 1 Thess 5:11; 4:18.

specific structure of accountability. It must insist that those seeking spiritual help from the church be held to the established standards of accountability without any deviation whatsoever.

One of the reasons for the need to place such rigid and specific structures of accountability on those guilty of sexual abuse is to protect them against themselves. The nature of the sin is so twisted and abnormal that the rate of recidivism (the tendency of a convicted criminal to reoffend) on the part of sex offenders is alarmingly high. Any reliable and objective source evaluating the pathology of sex offenders verifies this reality. Consequently, those in the church who seek to help such people and who adopt a distinctly Christian approach to the counseling should not assume that counseling from a biblical point of view somehow precludes the possibility of recidivism. This is true even when a former sex abuser makes a very genuine confession of faith demonstrable by good works. The fact is that the mechanisms of normalcy and the barriers that won't even allow such thoughts to enter the mind of most people have completely broken down in the thinking of a sexual abuser. Building walls of accountability to help them to never cross such boundaries again are needed and helpful. But to assume, especially in cases where an adult person had a past pattern of abuse, that they can be entirely freed from such impulses is mistaken, with potentially catastrophic results.

The Center for Sex Offender Management goes to great lengths to underscore this reality. As part of a systematic review of adult and juvenile sex offender management strategies, they warn about the dangers of a subjective approach in assessing risk factors as opposed to a more empirical, data-based approach.

Estimating recidivism risk is perhaps the most common assessment issue raised during the sex offender management process. Indeed, risk estimates can be useful for informing many key decisions with adult and juvenile sex offenders, such as disposition or sentencing, the type of placement or required level of care, release from facilities, and the application of registration and community notification policies. Assessing risk is particularly helpful for guiding decisions about which individuals will benefit most from interventions and strategies that are both time and resource intensive (e.g., prison-based or residential sex offender treatment, intensive supervision, and ancillary accountability measures such as electronic monitoring). The purely subjective, and therefore inconsistent, nature of this assessment strategy (Unstructured Clinical Judgment) means that different assessors may reach very different conclusions about a given offender. Because the potential implications of inaccurate assessments and the associated management decisions with sex offenders are significant (e.g., additional victims in the community, restricted liberties of an offender), all attempts should be made to increase the reliability of risk assessments within the context of sex offender management. Therefore, the exclusive use of unstructured clinical judgment is largely inadvisable.[6]

---

[6] The Center for Sex Offender Management, Accessed July 20, 2023, https://cepp.com/project/center-for-sex-offender-management-csom/

Likewise, uninformed, unstructured, and ill-conceived measures of accountability placed among former abusers within the church are not only "largely inadvisable"; they are totally unbiblical.

PROBATION: Demanding the Needed Time to Ensure Containment

Closely aligned with the need for accountability is a specified period of probation. It is vital that those guilty of sexual abuse undergo a lengthy period of testing and observing both their conduct and character. The period of the probation must take into consideration the details of the case (distance of age between the abused and abuser, the severity of the abuse, and the duration of the abuse). All these things determine when and if a past abuser can be released from the monitoring supervision demanded by the probation. In some cases, based on the facts of the case and the wisdom of the church leadership, especially when a person fully submits to the structures of accountability and probation and proves themselves trustworthy over time, they may be released from probation. In other cases, because of the specifics and severity of the sin, a person must remain under church probation for the duration of their life.

An astoundingly interesting fact of church history is that the earliest Christians were forced to deal with a controversy roughly related to probation for those guilty of gross sin. The controversy revolved around when and if Christians who had slipped back into idolatry should be restored and readmitted to the church.

THE CRITICAL NEED FOR CONTAINMENT

During the time of Cyprian, one of the martyred bishops of the third century, many confessing Christians succumbed to the temptation to fall back into idol worship. Due to the Decian persecution (249–251), regarded to be the first coordinated empire-wide persecution of the church, Christians were threatened with death if they did not sacrifice to the gods. Consequently, scores of confessing believers succumbed to the pressure and appeared to have totally apostatized. Since some of them later repented and sought to be reconciled to the church, the question forced influential church leaders to wrestle with the basis on which such people could be restored to the church. In the book, *A Concise History of Christian Thought*, Tony Lane summarizes the questions with which the early church wrestled. There was no clear consensus, and it became a point of significant controversy.

> Traditionally, those who had apostatized (renounced their faith) were not readmitted into the church. There were two separate issues. First, should the lapsed be readmitted at once, *or* only after a time of penance (public confession followed by a period of austere penitence), *or* never? Secondly, who was to decide this question? Those who were imprisoned for their faith, and ready to die for it (the confessors) were taking it upon themselves to reconcile the lapsed to the church. There was some traditional warrant for their action, but some were acting irresponsibly, lavishing 'pardons' on all and sundry. Did this authority lie with the confessors or the bishops? Cyprian insisted that the right lay

with the bishops, though they were to heed the recommendations of the confessors. Cyprian wrote an important work, *The Lapsed*, addressing this question. After the persecution, a council at Carthage in 251 decided that reconciliation was possible for the lapsed, after a period or penance. The following year, in the face of possible renewed persecution, another council decided that all who had at once begun penance would be readmitted forthwith. Cyprian took a leading role at these councils.[7]

While the particular sin to which the early church was responding (gross idolatry) is different from that of sexual abuse, the point of similarity is unquestionable; when should a confessing Christian who has sinned in such a vile way, yet repented and sought restoration to the church, be readmitted? While all the above cautions must be considered, the early church, conditioned on genuine repentance and a time of proving themselves, exemplified the gospel ethic of balancing forgiveness and restoration against a needed accountability.

CONSEQUENCES: The Willingness to Allow the Sowing and Reaping Process Time to Enhance Containment

To enhance containment, it is essential that there be a willingness to allow the full array of consequences to fall on the

---

[7] Tony Lane, *A Concise History of Christian Thought* (Grand Rapids, MI: Baker Academic, 1992), 25.

guilty. While the impulses of Christian grace and forgiveness desire the full recovery of the guilty, as we do in cases of our own personal sin, we must refuse a sentimental reaction that would stand in the way of an abuser fully reaping the consequences of their sin. "Do not be deceived, God is not mocked; for whatever a man sows, this he will also reap. For the one who sows to his own flesh will from the flesh reap corruption, but the one who sows to the Spirit will from the Spirit reap eternal life" (Gal 6:7–8). However, because of the understandable struggle a victim of abuse may have forgiving an abuser and the natural tendency to want to retaliate, we must ensure that the consequences meted out for sin are those determined by God, not man.

If the person guilty of such abuse is a true believer, rest assured that a divine set of consequences for such sin has been irresistibly set into motion. "For those whom the Lord loves he disciplines, and he scourges every son whom he receives" (Heb 12:6). The guilty will not only experience the divine chastisement, but they will feel acutely both the pain of a conscience tortured by such willful sin and the blows of the Holy Spirit sent for the conviction of such sin. Ralph Waldo Emerson's descript commentary on the law of consequences for sin provides a clear window into what is most deeply felt by the guilty—

> Sow a thought and you reap an action; sow an act and you reap a habit; sow a habit and you reap a character; sow a character and you reap a destiny.

Sins of the magnitude of sexual abuse do not arise in a person out of nowhere and blow up in a mere moment of time. Such sins always involve a process of thinking that starts in the mind, but it does not end in the mind. It advances from mind to action to habit; until it is deeply entrenched in character. By the grace of the gospel of Jesus Christ alone, on the condition of confession and repentance, it does not need to eventuate in a destiny. The earthly consequences, however, are unavoidable. The more sin is indulged, the more deeply it digs a trench in the ground of our mind. Part of the God-determined consequences for sin involves the guilty person admitting, because of their own choices, the undeniable reality of such a process. As the old saying goes, "you reap WHAT you sow, you reap AFTER you sow, and you reap MORE than you sow." Sad as it is, willful sexual sins have the power to enslave! They have an unusual power to bring the person under their dominion. "Also keep back Your servant from presumptuous sins; Let them not rule over me" (Ps 19:13a). By God's inscrutable purposes and mercy, the very process of reaping WHAT, MORE, and AFTER we have sown becomes a tool of chastisement that makes certain the pain and reality of consequences. In cases of sexual abuse, the full magnitude of consequences must be allowed to play out.

A vital part of the practical side of allowing an abuser to feel the full consequences for their actions, along with not mediating to lessen any legal incarceration, is to demand a process of counseling that fully explores the roots of their sin. This is uncomfortable for both the counselor and the abuser, but it is essential. Probing deeply into what stood at the root of the sin is a necessary part of the consequences for sin. To the best of a counselor's ability, fully exposing what led the person to act in such an immensely inappropriate sexual way is critical to ensuring such conduct is corrected and that such tendencies are rightly managed within the church. This forces the abuser to look deeply within himself to deal honestly with any remaining vestiges of perverted desire. It requires regularly scheduled meetings with the pastor (or other skilled counselors) sufficient to thoroughly deal with all the elements involved in the sin.

One further point should be made regarding the need to allow the consequences for our sin to work a transforming and purifying grace in our lives. Cheap, uninformed, and undiscerning applications of "forgiveness" can weaken, if not obliterate, the needed role of consequences. Commenting on the pattern of abuse that David endured at the hands of the fickle and impenitent King Saul, Walter Chantry made an astute observation—

> Readiness to forgive those who say, "I repent," is a duty. To put the matter behind one's back and to seek no further judicial recourse for an injury from that moment is required of those who forgive. However, the repair of trust when broken is not so easily accomplished. Nor is it required that anyone expose himself to further injury after he has been seriously and repeatedly hurt by the hands of one who has shown himself "unstable." Churches and Christian counselors go too far when they insist that forgiveness requires returning to former relationships as though nothing

has broken them. Forgiveness does not require the injured to risk more of the same mistreatment in friendship, marriage, or business. In these days we hear of too many unwise pressures which are brought upon injured parties in the name of forgiveness. There may come a time when men must go separate ways: "David went his way, and Saul returned to his place."[8]

The Rule of the Church: Stop Regurgitating Spoiled Food

Many of the arguments of this book have moved from general principles to more specific applications. To implement the principle of containment as best as possible when cases of abuse surface in the church, we must apply a general principle for church discipline to specific cases of sexual abuse. In general, when gross personal sin on the part of a Christian becomes public knowledge and requires church-wide notification, correction, or even excommunication, the rule is to deal with it thoroughly in the present but to come to a point in the near future when the church ceases to talk about it. The teaching of Scripture demands that such sin not be "hushed" or "swept under a rug." In the interest of the purity of the church and the testimony of our Savior, it must be dealt with in a biblical manner. However, when the biblical requirements for dealing

---

[8] Walter J. Chantry, *David: Man of Prayer, Man of War* (Edinburgh, UK: The Banner of Truth Trust, 2007, 2015), 108.

with it have been fulfilled, other biblical requirements demand that we put it in the past.

Typically, when gross sin demands open discussion in the church in order to faithfully carry out Scripture's demand for discipline, numerous things are done: 1) Open discussion of the sin is limited to members who make up the church family. 2) All nonmembers are dismissed for the detailed conversation along which church discipline must be processed (An exception to this is justified in severe cases of sin that become public knowledge throughout the community). 3) All those under the age of membership (or younger minors) are dismissed from the meeting. 4) Once notification has been made and church discipline carried out, the church is normally encouraged to put it in the past, forgive and restore like God does. The church family is encouraged to cease talking about it, even among themselves. All these actions are encouraged because this is exactly how God deals with our sins when they are confessed. He forgives and He forgets! He does not hang them over our head and rehearse them in our ears repeatedly. He moves past them and asks us to do the same. Containment of sin is a principle modeled by God and it is the pattern we should seek to emulate. It may titillate the sinful heart to rehearse the sins of others and satisfy a rather devilish desire, but it works against the principle of containment that seeks to insulate others from further contamination. "For lack of wood the fire goes out, and where there is no whisperer, contention quiets down. Like charcoal to hot embers and wood to fire, so is a contentious man to kindle strife. The words of a whisperer are like dainty morsels, and they go down into the innermost parts of the body" (Prov 26:20–22).

A good example of the need to openly talk about an important issue and then to intentionally cease talking about it is when a dating couple moves to the stage of serious intentions about marriage. It is natural and quite normal for a person to wonder and question the sexual past of their potential marriage partner. After all, marriage binds them in covenant to share with their partner that which is never shared with another person. While others may disagree, as a pre-marital counselor with many logged hours talking with young couples about their fears and concerns about future marriage, I believe they have every right to know about their potential partners past sexual activity. Since trust is an essential pillar on which a healthy relationship stands, couples must be completely honest with one another about this aspect of their life. If there are issues of sin that preceded the marriage, it allows the couple to fully and transparently deal with those issues ahead of time. It gives them the opportunity, by honesty, confession if needed, and forgiveness to apply the ethic of the gospel at the very outset of their marriage. The key, however, is what is advised past the initial transparency and open discussion. I tell the couple the reason they need to bring it up now is so you never have to bring it up again. It is dealt with and never needs discussion again. If there are sinful regrets in the past, they are left in the past, not brought up again, and are never thrown in the face of your partner.

THE CRITICAL NEED FOR CONTAINMENT

	Points of Practical Pastoral Wisdom
Primary Goal	In the fifth stage of applying the ethic of the gospel to cases of sexual abuse, the pastor-counselor must strain every nerve to provide for and ensure that the sin is contained within the spectrum of what is appropriate.
Real Life Examples	While serving as an elder of a large church during my seminary days and while serving as the senior pastor of two smaller churches, cases of abuse, differing in degree of severity, arose in the churches. In all cases, clearly outlined parameters were thoughtfully developed and implemented with discretion, all to ensure the protection of others, the testimony of the church, and the integrity of the gospel.
Vital Questions	Do you understand and agree with the decision of the church leadership to exercise the forms of discipline your sin requires (their agreement and consent is essential if they are to have the right of continued attendance)? Do you agree to live under the restrictions being placed upon you completely and consistently? Do you understand why the Scriptures make these steps necessary?
Typical Counselee Responses	Those guilty of pedophilia as adults tend to want to talk about their past sins in a way that can quickly deteriorate and become immensely

	unhealthy. While the sin and its specific manifestations (along with diagnosing root causes) need to be discussed during the initial times of the revelation, twisted sinful minds sometimes derive a sense of perverted delight in repeating their crime during counseling. The pastor/counselor must be aware of this at the outset, detect the signs when it begins to happen, and to refuse it altogether. **NOTE**: Remember that the rates of recidivism among adult men guilty of pedophilia is exceptionally high. Awareness of this tendency must, sadly but necessarily, be kept in view.
Specific Applications	Principles of accountability (while recognizing the limitations) must be vigorously enforced when attempting to help those guilty of sexual deviancy. **Constant monitoring** by men aware of the deviancy is essential. Women should monitor as well when the abuser is a woman (far rarer) or when a woman was necessarily a part of the circle of those informed about the abuse. **Severe limitations** that never allow a past abuser to be in the nursery, among children, among those in the youth group, among college aged attenders, or ever in the bathroom without an accountability partner. **Regularly scheduled reviews** must take place and, in some cases, must carry on for the duration of the time an abuser continues to attend the church.
Homework	**Scripture memorization** must be constant to help past abusers "stay" their mind on that which is true, honorable, just, pure, lovely, and

commendable (Phil 4:8). Even this, essential as it is, is not a sure-proof means of total victory; just as it is not a sure-proof means of preventing sins among those who have never once been tempted to abuse another person, but who struggle with sins like impatience, a lack of trust in God, covetousness, or lust. Whenever possible (financial ability being a consideration) an abuser should be strongly encouraged to regularly consult biblical and trusted secular counselors who deal with these behavioral disorders continually, are true specialists, and who understand the pathologies of such persons simply because of the massive case file they have.

CHAPTER 7

The Call for CLOSURE: Wiping Away the Tears

Picking Up the Pieces

Is it possible to apply the ethic of the gospel of Christ in a way that effectually brings real closure to victims of sexual abuse? Can full disclosure, justice, confession, forgiveness, and containment, advanced along the lines of the gospel, come even remotely close to terminating all the grief, bitterness, sadness, anger, and confusion experienced by a victim of sexual abuse? Can the atoning work of Jesus Christ effectually dry the years of tears that have flowed down the cheeks of victims of abuse? Even when perpetrators are prosecuted to the full extent of the law and the abused are given every assurance their abusers will spend ample time in prison, can they experience something greater than what is often expressed as the best possible outcome—"at least no one will ever suffer at the hands of your abuser again"? Can victims of such sinful offenses rise above a mere satisfaction derived by knowing their abusers have got their just deserts? Can an internal healing take place deep within the heart of the abused because it is pursued, not along the lines of raw justice, but because it is experienced by the operative power of God's unmerited grace? The gospel promises it can!

Jeremiah cried out to the Lord: "Heal me, O LORD, and I will be healed; Save me and I will be saved, For You are my praise" (Jer 17:14). The healing work of Jesus Christ is always pulled in the wake of His saving work. "Surely our griefs He Himself bore, and our sorrows He carried. . . . But He was pierced through for our transgressions, He was crushed for our iniquities; The chastening for our well-being fell upon Him, And by His scourging we are healed" (Isa 53:4–5). While every physical ailment is given no absolute assurance to be healed in this life, the gospel of Christ makes every provision for our complete spiritual healing—a need far greater than any bodily ailment: "and He Himself bore our sins in His body on the cross. . . for by His wounds you were healed" (1 Pet 2:24). "The LORD is near to the brokenhearted and saves those who are crushed in spirit" (Ps 34:18). Ultimately, through the triumphs of Christ's work through the gospel, every tear shed in the heart of every sinner will be dried—eradicated and terminated forever! "Behold, the tabernacle of God is among men, and He will dwell among them, and they shall be His people, and God Himself will be among them, and He will wipe away every tear from their eyes; and there will no longer be any death; there will no longer be any mourning, or crying, or pain; the first things have passed away" (Rev 21:3–4).

It is granted that the complete closure, total termination, and the wiping away of every tear due to sin must wait till the dawn of eternity and the full consummation of all things in Christ. But the gospel, the very genius by which God has made such promise, is at work in the present "now"! The genius of God's gospel alone can apply a healing balm with enough miraculous power sufficient to salve the wound left by abuse. Victims of sexual abuse are sacred vessels who are forced to pick up the many pieces of their life shattered by their assailants. They must process through an ugly array of feelings brought on by their abusers: PTSD, the double trauma of rehearsing the initial trauma, reliving the horror over and over again, responding to inept, negligent, or unwilling legal help, self-blame and self-loathing, a continued sense of violation of privacy, repressed memories, the need to relabel themselves, and the irresistible urge to regain a sense of identity by the re-scripting of their own life narrative. These are only a sampling of the burdens born in the aftermath of sexual abuse. Can the gospel heal people bruised, battered, and broken in such ways?

Putting the Past Behind You

One of the recurring motifs among those seeking to help victims of abuse is to move them past the status of victim to being a survivor. There is no doubt that some overcome the status of victimhood, but whose status as a survivor remains tenuous at best. Applying the healing balm of the gospel is alone capable of moving a person far beyond mere survival. It promises more than surviving. Putting the past behind you on the order of the gospel truly affects a personal thriving. The operation of the principles of the gospel at work in the heart of the abused can move them beyond victim and survivor status—all the way to being a triumphant overcomer. "But in all these things we overwhelmingly conquer through Him who loved us. For I am convinced that neither death, nor life, nor angels, nor principalities, nor things present, nor things to come, nor powers, nor height, nor depth, nor any other created thing, will be able to separate us from the love of God, which is in Christ Jesus our Lord" (Rom 8:37–39).

Since closure refers "to a feeling that an emotional or traumatic experience has been resolved," great care must be taken in applying this term as a desired outcome for victims of sexual abuse. Is it reasonable to expect that the gospel possesses the power to resolve the emotional trauma set into motion by sexual abuse? From the standpoint of memory alone, can a victim ever be expected to totally purge such an event from their memory in the same way they might permanently erase a minor spelling error off a piece of white paper? Hardly! The question then, put more in scriptural terms, is what we are to do with the indelible imprint left on the memory by sin? How, in the words of the apostle Paul, does a person experience the spiritual genius of "forgetting what lies behind and reaching forward to what lies ahead" (Phil 3:13)? We might view this "forgetting the past" and "reaching to the future" mindset as the equivalent of "spiritual closure." While I firmly believe only the gospel can produce this kind of closure, some feel that attempts at closure are futile and a slight against victims of abuse. I sympathize with this sentiment without endorsing it whole heartedly.

Nancy Berns, speaker, professor of sociology, and author of *Closure: The Rush to End Grief and What It Costs Us,* articulates this view with some rather insightful observations. In 2011, just following the revelation of the Jerry Sandusky, Penn State sexual abuse debacle, she wrote—

> Hoping that victims will find "closure" in the Penn State sex abuse scandal is wrong. Using the concept of closure helps those responsible for the harm; it doesn't help victims. What does "closure for victims" really mean when used in these political and criminal cases? . . . Victims of sexual assault do not get closure. Effects from abuse stay with people the rest of their lives. This does not mean that victims cannot go on to have successful and beautiful lives. Many do. But they still carry the pain from the abuse. Other victims don't recover but are lost to severe depression, drugs, or suicide. . . . We want to believe victims can find closure. Don't misunderstand what I mean. Victims can heal and learn to live with the experience. But when we fool ourselves into thinking they have "closure," then the devastating, long-term effects of abuse do not stay in the conversation.[1]

No one can read such an observation and dismiss it out of hand as if it contains no element of truth. However, through the application of the ethic of the gospel, "the devastating, long-term

---

[1] Nancy Berns, "'Closure' Harms Sexual Assault Victims," *Nancy Berns Blog*, November 9 2011, http://www.nancyberns.com/%E2%80%9Cclosure%E2%80%9D-harms-sexual-assault-victims.html.

effects of abuse" stay in the conversation for sure, but they stay in the conversation through the language of the gospel. The language of the gospel reflects the heart and essence of the gospel. The heart and essence of the gospel testifies to a world of sinners who are all guilty and all who deserve the just condemnation of their sin. The heart and essence of the gospel testifies to the infinite grace of God that sent His Son to die in the place of such guilty sinners. The heart and essence of the gospel provides free forgiveness to all who will confess and repent of their sin. The answer to what we must do with the indelible imprint left on the memory by sin is that we do with the greatest of sins what we do with those sins regarded to be the least of all sins. We apply the gospel! The gospel is not a gospel for little sins only. It is a gospel for the sins of the whole world. The answer to what we must do with the indelible imprint left on the memory by sin is that we regard the sins of others against us as God has regarded our sins against Him. We forgive completely! We forget as best we can! And when the memories of our own sins haunt us and the memories of sins committed against us anger us, we preach the message of the gospel to ourselves. This requires far more than the discipline of sheer determination. It swings on the hinges of faith and nothing else. It is the genius of the gospel.

A personal testimony from my own life might help to outline a strategy for "forgetting the past." There is nothing juicy and scandalous to tell and nothing even remotely close to the trauma brought about by sexual offenses. It is not the story of a one-time event in which someone sinned against me or a case of me sinning against another, though such occurrences have happened repeatedly in my life as a Christian. The strategy is what I refer to as "moments of clarity." Moments of clarity suggest a way to fight the death-dealing effects of sin that explode repeatedly in the life of a Christian and upset the health of the body and the sanity of the soul and spirit. These moments of clarity do not come out of nowhere but are the result of a decided effort to get alone with God in a communion with Him that turns the mind in the right direction. Allow me to elaborate.

The Christian drama is a life-long, struggle to the death with sin. It is warfare. Each day is a walk through a spiritual minefield. Every true Christian knows this reality. Life is a crucible patterned after the life of our Savior. As He carried the cross of sin to His death, so we are called to share in His suffering. On the emotional level, the way this plays out is that sin sometimes gets the upper hand, wins the battle, and leaves the Christian flat on his face in a muddled mass of guilt, shame, and despair. God is so infinitely holy in His essence that an inevitable law is set into motion when the Christian willfully acquiesces to sin. We come to times in our life when, because of sin, "the whole head is sick and the whole heart is faint. From the sole of the foot even to the head there is nothing sound in it, only bruises, welts and raw wounds, not pressed out or bandaged, or softened with oil" (Isa 1:5–6). Now I ask, what has God ordained to mollify the wounds produced by sin? The answer, plain and simple is the beauty of the all-healing GOSPEL! What I have found personally, when sin has worked its soul crushing effects on me (I'm sure experienced by other

Christians), is that getting alone with God in long prayer and deep meditation of Scripture brings these "moments of clarity." I could not live without them. The goodness and grace of God, ministered by the Holy Spirit, perceived by the meek reception of Scripture's message, and received by faith's grip of all the benefits of the gospel received in prayer is what God has ordained to bring about such moments of clarity.

Without experiencing on the personal level what a victim of sexual abuse must go through, it is essential that they experience the same kind of moments of clarity in coming to a sound and healthy mental response to their affliction. Without question, Christians who have endured such trauma have to struggle with the sins committed against them. But without doubt they must also struggle, deep in the unfathomable depths of the human spirit, with their own deplorable sins. What they need is the moments of clarity the message of the gospel preaches to them and to all mankind.

Reaching for a Hopeful Future

In a 2017 Washington Post article, Kathryn Leehane wrote a courageous piece chronicling not only the sexual abuse she endured at the hands of a high school teacher, but also the entire failure of the school administration and the local police to prosecute her case in a just way. As a result, she struggled for years in ways too painful for anyone to understand other than those who have been forced to walk her path. In particular, she

THE CALL FOR CLOSURE

describes her elusive effort to find closure and a sense of personal peace—

> The passing years, however, did not bring me peace. Two decades later, I still found myself thinking about the abuse. The scenes in the teacher's office played on an endless loop, and I felt dirty, used, helpless. The images plagued me. The what-ifs haunted me. The injustice infuriated me. And the hashtags and the stories and the survivor language couldn't change that. My abuser recently died; his body succumbed to cancer. My skin prickled again upon hearing the news, but this time, as I breathed out, I felt a calm sweep over me. I would no longer need to carry this load. While mourners celebrated his life, I celebrated his death. Knowing he'd never hurt anyone again was a gift, allowing me—finally—to find closure.[2]

Is the death of an abuser the only way for a victim of abuse to find closure? Must an abuser, even after their death, continue to hold the victim of their abuse in a life-long bondage? With the greatest caution and deepest sense of personal limitations, may I suggest the most optimistic possibility—when those victimized by abuse apply the ethic of the gospel very personally to themselves, it will not leave them with a half-sized, partial

---

[2] Kathryn Leehane, "When the Legal System Fails Sexual Assault Victims, We Have to Find Our Own Closure," *The Washington Post*, October 20, 2017, https://www.washingtonpost.com/outlook/the-courts-regularly-fail-sexual-assault-victims-so-we-have-to-find-our-own-closure/2017/10/20/d476099a-b42d-11e7-be94-fabb0f1e9ffb_story.html.

closure and healing that is possible only upon the death of their abuser. The closure was secured at the cross and can be personally harnessed by faith that grips the significance of the death of Christ—both to you the victim and to the person who so wrongfully victimized you. By faith, don't allow yourself to feel like the only way you can cease carrying the load of this burden is by the death of your abuser. You may stop carrying the load of this burden by allowing the death of your Savior to carry the burdensome load. He did this when He bore your sins on the cross. He did this when He bore the sins of your abuser. "Come to Me, all who are weary and heavy-laden, and I will give you rest. Take My yoke upon you and learn from Me, for I am gentle and humble in heart, and you will find rest for your souls. For My yoke is easy and My burden is light" (Matt 11:28–30).

It is not surprising that victims of sexual abuse often become the most zealous advocates for others so abused. Their goal is the protection and healing of others; protection to prevent others from experiencing such horror. Healing in order that their personal experience of victory might be passed on to others. Moore writes,

> Some of the most compassionate advocates for children I know were emotionally or physically or sexually abused themselves as children. They survived and spend their lives making sure no one else will go through the same trauma. . . . Often, those who live through such things are more proactive than their peers at putting good practices in place ahead of time.[3]

If the story line of this book is anything, it is that the surest way to successfully advocate for others is to follow the advocacy of Jesus Christ modeled in the gospel. "My dear children, I write this to you so that you will not sin. But if anybody does sin, we have an advocate with the Father—Jesus Christ, the Righteous One. He is the atoning sacrifice for our sins, and not only for ours but also for the sins of the whole world" (1 John 2:1–2). It is only when we grip by faith that Jesus' death on the cross provided an atoning sacrifice for "our" sins, the death of the just for the unjust, that we have discovered the genius by which to cover the sins "others" have sinned against us.

One of the most, if not the most successful lawyers of all time was Sir Lionel Alfred Luckhoo. His reputation earned him an entry in the Guinness Book of Records (1990) where he is dubbed the world's "most successful lawyer." He was famed for some 245 consecutive successful acquittals in murder cases. He was born in British Guiana (now known as Guyana), and later served as a judge of the Supreme Court of Guyana. In a biography of Sir Lionel Luckhoo, Fred Archer described part of his courtroom technique. In advising younger criminal defense lawyers regarding a jury member not being convinced by the arguments, he advised—

> Concentrate on him, look him in the eye, make him feel that you are ignoring everything else to hold his attention because the life of your client is in his hands and that he

---

[3] Russell Moore, *The Storm-Tossed Family: How the Cross Reshapes the Home* (Nashville, TN: B&H Publishing Group, 2018), 43.

must be convinced, as he ought to be convinced, that your man is innocent and deserves an acquittal.[4]

Can we really believe, based on Christ's righteousness and atoning death for our sins, that we can be declared innocent? This is what the gospel promises. Since we believe the gospel can make us innocent, when we know ourselves to be guilty in the extreme, we must believe He can do the same for others—even the worst of sinners. "Do not be deceived; neither fornicators, nor idolaters, nor adulterers, nor effeminate, nor homosexuals, nor thieves, nor the covetous, nor drunkards, nor revilers, nor swindlers, will inherit the kingdom of God. **Such were some of you**; but you were washed, but you were sanctified, but you were justified in the name of the Lord Jesus Christ and in the Spirit of our God" (1 Cor 6:9–11).

We must grip this reality about our great advocate—Jesus Christ the Righteous. Every client in the hands of Jesus is a vile sinner. It is the eyes of the all-holy God into which Jesus looks and pleads for His clients. He does not try to convince God by clever or shady argument of the innocence of those clearly guilty. He there presents as an argument the merits of His own atoning sacrifice, and by this argument alone, God can declare perfectly innocent and righteous those as guilty as sin. His advocacy is unfailing! Christ stood up before God and continues to stand up before Him to intercede for us, to be our mediator, to be the arbitrator and go between for sinful man and holy God. His

---

[4] Fred Archer, *Sir Lionel* (Costa Mesa, CA: Gift Publications, 1980), 33.

advocacy is not reserved for the best, there is none. It is freely offered to the worst, which encompasses all of us! His advocacy is the termination for all the guilt and sorrow of our sin.

	Points of Practical Pastoral Wisdom
Primary Goal	In the final stage of applying the ethic of the gospel to cases of sexual abuse, the pastor-counselor must compassionately urge the counselee to fully embrace the provisions of the gospel to bring the effects of sin to resolution and closure.
Real Life Examples	As scandalous and seemingly impossible as it is to humanly conceived ideas, God's grace abundantly triumphs over all of sins worst effects— "where sin abounded, grace did much more abound" (Rom 5:20). Christians who have fallen into gross moral sin, the consequences of which appear to be permanently destructive, through the grace of God and the application of the ethic of the gospel can come out on the other side spiritually stronger after their failure than they were before. Amazing Grace! More often than is realized, a sad form of self-reliance and self-righteousness embeds itself deep in the psyche of some Christians. In such cases, to remove every vestige of self-righteousness and reveal just how sinful and broken they are, it takes the magnitude of a great moral fall to reveal it. It is only after seeing more clearly the violation of God's righteous Law and the penetrating conviction of

	sin that reveal the enormity of their sin. It is only then that they are in a condition to fully receive the grace of God. Only after broken and deeply humbled by the exposure of their sin do they see the significance of God's grace. It is only then that it takes full hold of them and revolutionizes their life in profound ways. In some cases, the person may come to the realization, after depression, suicidal impulses, and a whole array of other efforts to fix themselves and assuage their guilt that they are not truly born again. It requires the depth of a fall of this magnitude to reveal the depth of the need and that only the forgiveness provided in Jesus can meet that need. Indeed, the glorious ethic of the gospel can bring true beauty out of an ash heap of sin. "Where sin increased, grace abounded all the more, so that, as sin reigned in death, grace also might reign through righteousness leading to eternal life through Jesus Christ our Lord" (Rom 5:20b–21).
Vital Questions	Do you believe God's grace in the gospel has enabled you to find closure and to put this awful episode of sin behind you? Do you want this kind of closure? Are you learning, despite the ravages of sin, that you can be an overcomer instead of a lifelong victim, or a lifelong victimizer? Do you believe that forgiveness through the gospel not only encourages you to bury the past but commands you to do so? What do you think is the secret to overcoming when the black lines of sin continue to

Typical Counselee Responses	indelibly imprint the memory of sin on your mind? The struggle to put sin in the past is often manifested by intense emotionalism, tears, anguish, stifling paralysis of soul, and a penchant to rehearse the sin *ad infinitum*. However, two words summarize the struggle of the abused and the abuser to move past sin and toward closure. They are the same as that with which we all struggle in the aftermath of our sin—GUILT and UNBELIEF! There is not a single psychological modality in the world that can relieve and soothe the conscience defiled by sin. The gospel modality alone can clear away the blood stain of sin. "The blood of Jesus Christ his Son cleanses us from all sin" (1 John 1:7).
Specific Applications	It is not apparent to me whether it is harder for an abused person to forgive their abuser or whether it is harder for the abuser to fully accept forgiveness—both divine and human forgiveness. I don't know. What I do know is that faith in the gospel, anchored deep in the heart by the work of Christ and the operation of the Holy Spirit, is able to give the full assurance of sins forgiven amid the darkest of sins. Christ's death satisfied the justice demanded by an infinitely holy and just God.
Homework	Though I have not recommended any books as part of assignments that might be of help to both the abused and abusers, there are many valuable books that will prove helpful to those inclined to read. One particularly valuable book that I highly

> recommend (cited earlier in the book) is co-authored by Ken Sande and Kevin Johnson—*Resolving Everyday Conflict*. In fact, I think it should be required reading for every minister of the gospel and Christian counselor. I cannot recommend it highly enough to those attempting to work through the ethic of the gospel as it meets human sin and conflict.

Conclusion

If there was ever a single case in Scripture where a person who was sinned against abominably and in a way that violated the social norms of the time, but who reacted by applying the ethic of the gospel to the person who offended him, it is Philemon. The book of the Bible that bears his name and the account of the plea the apostle Paul made to him to forgive his offender along the lines of the gospel is a pure example of a Christian fusing the ethic of the gospel with his behavior. It is the very essence of Christianity in practice. The book of Philemon, one of only four one-chapter books in the Bible, is a message from the apostle Paul strenuously appealing to a first century slave owner to apply the genius of the gospel to the criminal actions of a runaway slave, Onesimus. It is an appeal to both forgive him and restore him.

The appeals are set forth directly in the letter to Philemon. *"Yet for love's sake I rather **appeal** to you. . . I **appeal** to you for my child Onesimus. . . If then you regard me a partner, **accept** him as you would me"* (Philem 9, 10,17). It is the basis and reasoning, however, upon which Paul makes the appeal that so eloquently applies the ethic of the gospel to a case of cultural sin as notorious as the sin of Onesimus. Before unfolding the verse that embodies Paul's use of the gospel ethic as an appeal to Philemon to forgive Onesimus, it is necessary to observe the kind of person Onesimus was as well as the seriousness of his sinful crime against Philemon. Onesimus was not only a runaway slave who broke Roman law (punishable by death), but he likely stole from Philemon and defrauded his owner in a way completely unacceptable in first century Rome. He was guilty of gross injustice and unrighteousness. "If he has **wronged** [unrighteousness] you in any way or **owes** [debt] you anything" (Philem 18). Charles Haddon Spurgeon, in a sermon entitled, "The Story of a Runaway Slave," gives this helpful and picturesque sketch of the character of Onesimus—

> He was a slave. In those days, slaves were very ignorant, untaught and degraded. Being barbarously used, they for the most part, themselves sunk in the lowest barbarism Neither did their masters attempt to raise them out of it. Love fixed itself upon this degraded being who was now mixed up with the very scum of society? And what the scum of society was in old Rome I should not like to think, for the upper classes were about as brutalized in their general habits as we can very well conceive! What the lowest scum of all must have been, none of us can tell. Onesimus was part and parcel of the dregs of a sink of sin. Onesimus was among the worst of the worst! And yet Eternal Love, which passed by kings and princes and left Pharisees and Sadducees, philosophers and

magi to stumble in the dark as they chose, fixed its eyes upon this poor benighted creature that he might be made a vessel to honor, fit for the Master's use!¹

Paul had evangelized Onesimus during his imprisonment in Rome and led him to confess faith in Christ. "I appeal to you for my child Onesimus, whom I have begotten in my imprisonment" (Philem 10). As one commentator noted, "In Onesimus we have a clear example of the kind of transformation that occurred in thousands of lives as the gospel message spread throughout the Roman Empire."² Philemon was a noted Christian in Colossae and a person in whose home Christians assembled for worship and instruction. Paul appealed to him to forgive and restore Onesimus on the genius and principle of the gospel, a gospel which Philemon knew to be the very basis upon which he could find forgiveness for his own sins. The glory of the gospel ethic brilliantly showcased in Philemon, which became the underlying principle by which Philemon was urged to forgive Onesimus, is expressed in Philemon 18—"But if he has wronged you in any way or owes you anything, **charge that to my account.**" The five words, "charge that to my account," have been described as "a brilliant cameo of gospel truth." Like a piece of jewelry with a profiled portrait carved on the background of a different material, Christ's work on the cross is

---

[1] Charles Haddon Spurgeon, "The Story of a Runaway Slave (1875)," *Metropolitan Tabernacle Pulpit*, vol. 21, reprint (London: Forgotten Books, 2018).

[2] "Introduction to Philemon," New International Version (Grand Rapids: Zondervan, 2017).

carved into this verse against the background of man's sin; in this case the background of not only the sin of Onesimus, but the sin of Philemon also. How does this verse condense the genius of the gospel in such a succinct statement? How would it immediately resonate with Philemon so that he understood Paul was admonishing him to forgive on the principle of the gospel? The words "charge that to my account" refer to the act of legally transferring the sin off the logbook of one person's record and on to another person's account. This is exactly what God did when he took the sins of all mankind and legally imputed them to Christ. "He made Him who knew no sin to be sin on our behalf, so that we might become the righteousness of God in Him" (2 Cor 5:21).

When Paul advised Philemon on this basis, he did not so much do it as a play on words, though that may have been involved. He did it because of his confidence that Philemon would interpret the words to be a clear allusion to exactly what God does with the sins of mankind through the death of Jesus Christ in the gospel. The threefold set of spiritual ideas compressed in this verse speak of debt, mediation, and payment. In the specific case at hand, Onesimus was debtor to Philemon, Paul was acting as a mediator, and he was willing to make whatever payment was necessary to satisfy the debt incurred by Onesimus, regardless of the cost: "I, Paul, am writing this with my own hand, I will repay it (not to mention to you that you owe to me even your own self as well)" (Philem 19). When this admonition rang in the ears of Philemon, he undoubtedly realized it was a cleverly inspired reference to the debt all men owe God due to their sin, the mediation of Christ, and His atoning sacrifice that took the full measure of punishment required by God's justice. Philemon was confronted with the need to apply the ethic of the gospel as freely and generously to Onesimus as God had applied it to him. Further, Paul took pains to drive home the idea of Christ's sacrificial death to provide eternal life for all men by suggesting that he, himself, acted according to the same genius of the gospel in his interactions with Philemon—"you owe to me even your own self as well."

This is the gospel! This is the gospel which only faith can receive. This is "the" distinctive Christian principle on which any person, regardless of the degree of sin committed against them, can freely and from the heart forgive all men their trespasses. "Freely you received, freely give" (Matt 10:8). "It is more blessed to give than to receive" (Acts 20:35). The mandate to forgive, issued to Philemon in the case of Onesimus, had great power; precisely because he had a sense of the magnitude of what was involved when God "charged" the guilt of his sin to Christ. It was this genius by which he could gladly forgive Onesimus. It is this genius, and this genius alone, by which the sad victim of sexual abuse may apply the gospel to their abuser.

Given that I am drawing on the sinful and degrading institution of slavery as an illustration for forgiveness, and since it was a slave who is presented in Scripture as having sinned against his owner, a needed caveat must be mentioned so the force and appropriateness of such arguments are not lost. The institution of slavery, practiced everywhere and throughout all human history up to this very time, is a great and unspeakable evil. We may all thank God that its termination in the western world is owed to the very ethic of the gospel so fervently advocated in this book. The abolitionist movement to end the slave trade, largely exemplified in the life and effort of William Wilberforce, was fueled by a distinctly Christian ethic. It is horrifically sad that it took so much time and pain to remove its vestiges from the United States. In the ancient world, however, no such scruples existed about slavery as an accepted aspect of social life.

Amazingly, the book of Philemon and the ethic of the gospel contained in it was a divine commentary on the value of human beings—even slaves were regarded at that time to be nothing more than property. While the book of Philemon is not a frontal assault on slavery, it set into motion the seeds of distinctly Christian thought that would place greater value on all human lives and propel the movement to end slavery. John MacArthur makes an astute comment on why New Testament Christianity postured itself toward the institution of slavery the way that it did—

> The NT nowhere directly attacks slavery; had it done so, the resulting slave insurrections would have been brutally suppressed and the message of the gospel hopelessly confused with that of social reform. Indeed, Christianity undermined the evils of slavery by changing the hearts of slaves and masters. By stressing the spiritual equality of

CONCLUSION

master and slave, the Bible did away with the evils of slavery's abuses.[3]

It is unarguable that the spiritual principle of freedom promised in the gospel became the inspiration for the emancipation of slaves. The gospel, with the principles of redemption and release inherent in its message, provides the foundation that drove the abolitionist's vision. Making the admonition to forgive along the lines of the ethic of the gospel as unfolded in Philemon, especially in cases of sexual sin, is done so with great hope. It is done with the hope that the same influence of the gospel may change deeply embedded attitudes about rightly helping people who have suffered sexual abuse in the same way its genius helped people suffering from the abuses of slavery. G. Campbell Morgan, in the *Analyzed Bible*, captures the theme of Philemon as "Christ and Social Relationships." He observes that Philemon "is a radiant revelation of the application of Christian principle to matters of individual life and social relationships."[4] My prayer for every person ever assaulted by sexual abuse is that they may find the genius of the gospel of Christ to be "a radiant revelation" of the best possible approach to deal with and to heal from such an offense. It can only happen by the application of the gospel of Christ.

---

[3] "Philemon: Bible Introductions," *Grace to You*, August 31, 2010. https://www.gty.org/library/bible-introductions/MSB57/philemon.
[4] G. Campbell Morgan, *The Analyzed Bible* (United States: Fleming H. Revell Company, 1907), 530–531.

Hypothetically, if an individual character in the New Testament had been specifically named as being a sexual abuser (and there is no doubt there is reference to such people coming to Christ),[5] no platitude of sentimental, cheap forgiveness would be advocated. In the case of Onesimus (the person guilty of sin), he was called upon to deal with his sin as a means of making it right with the one against whom he had sinned. His is the story of a criminal who was not left to wallow in his sin nor to excuse it by placing the blame on others. He was called to take very deliberate measures to make it right along the lines of the gospel. Thankfully, because of his conversion, he quite literally did a complete 180-degree-turnaround, both spiritually and physically. Spiritually, in that his entire life changed after being won to Christ by Paul while in prison; and physically he did a complete turn-around in that he was made to travel nearly thirteen hundred miles the opposite direction, walking and sailing from Rome back to Colossae, where he had violated the trust of Philemon. He did this to make things right in accordance with the ethic of the gospel.

The principles of Christianity make it clear that in order to deal with excessive sin in a way pleasing to God and in conformity to His Word and will, it must be prosecuted along the lines of the gospel: 1) full disclosure, 2) a demand for legal and ecclesiastical punishment, 3) full confession and repentance on the part of the offender, 4) the offer and extension of forgiveness after the model of God according the ethic of the

---

[5] 1 Cor 5:1; 2 Cor 6:9–11; Gal 5:19–21; 1 Tim 1:10.

CONCLUSION

gospel, 5) the critical need to contain the damage done by the sin, and 6) a biblical approach to wiping away the sorrow of sin and moving the abused forward in the best way possible. This approach does not sugarcoat, minimize, or trivialize the sin of abuse—it applies the healing balm of the all-potent gospel. Onesimus is an exemplar of the whole inhumaneness of the institution of slavery. His story is also a model for how the master of the gospel, Jesus Christ the Lord, is the genius whose power can transform entire social structures.

A friend of mine and colleague in ministry, along with his wife, were both the sad victims of abuse while growing up. In frank and laudable transparency, he shared with me his struggle to come to peace of heart through the gospel. In an unpublished paper, based on a sermon he preached, he relates a part of his testimony—

> When I rose in the morning it was to hate. When I lied down to sleep I couldn't because I couldn't turn the hate off until Jesus made all things new in me (2 Cor 5:17). Maybe you've been asking for healing when it isn't healing you need at all, but brokenness. I know you think you feel the burden of your abuser's sin, but friend, it is not your abuser's sin or anyone else's sin that's tearing you and your family apart. It is yours. I was taken to 14 therapists in 2 years. This was a total waste in every way except that they got paid for their time. But when I stopped striving and simply cried out, "Father I can't do this anymore, please take this burden from me," Oh brothers and sisters I can't

express the joy. I had freedom and a radically changed heart! If you need something to do, do this; throw yourself upon the mercy of a Holy God and wait for His answer. Repentance literally means a change of mind. It is a turning away from sin and a turning toward Christ. But these actions are simultaneous. Turning away from sin is only possible if you turn toward Christ and if you truly turn toward Christ you will turn from sin. But repentance ultimately must not be thought of only in terms of doing. Repentance is the gift of God granted because of the "kindness of God" (Rom 2:4). Here's how repentance works; think of any number of cheesy romance movies you've seen where the girl and guy end up at the airport terminal at the last minute to embrace the love they had previously refused. She's standing there holding her bags when she sees him. What does she do? She drops her luggage and embraces the one she loves. She lets go of her baggage and clings to him.[6]

It may be that you, an abuser, are carrying around the baggage of shame and guilt and are simply incapable of loosening the grip. You have an infestation of perversity engrained in your nature so deeply that is breeds every imaginable manner of disease. You may have been the longtime victim of abuse yourself and the sad reality that you have perpetuated the awful cycle and

---

[6] Austin Hetsler, "The All Sufficiency of Christ: A Biblical Prescription for Breaking the Bonds of Sexual Abuse, Physical Abuse, and Emotional Abuse," sermon.

CONCLUSION

become an abuser yourself is an ugly reality you cannot deny. To do so would prove you to be a liar and worse still, it is to make God a liar. "If we say that we have not sinned, we make Him a liar and His word is not in us" (1 John 1:10). You have likely made repeated, futile attempts to rid your soul of this one dark blot. If you could scrape it away with shards of glass, you would do so in a millisecond. But stains of this magnitude are spiritual in nature and there is only one remedy in the world that can remove your degraded sin and cleanse your vile heart—the gospel of Christ! You need to repent in the biblical sense of the word. Repentance is not a determination to self-reform; it is the change of mind that views your sin exactly as does God. It is the repentance needed by all sinners. Hand in hand with such God-granted repentance is faith in the only sacrifice that can atone for your sin. While turning in abject grief away from the atrocities of your sin, the gospel also commands a turning to Jesus Christ and the full acceptance of the Lamb of God. He will save you! "Behold, the Lamb of God who takes away the sin of the world!" (John 1:29). He will forgive you! "Take courage, son; your sins are forgiven" (Matt 9:2).

It may be that you, the abused, are carrying around the baggage of hatred and bitterness. For every resolution to let it go, it clings to you with a tenacity that seems omnipotent. You may be completely innocent, and the abuse committed against you is something for which you had no control and for which you are not responsible in any way. What you are responsible for is how you respond. You may seethe forever as if you are a pot of water over a flame that keeps you boiling with resentment, anger, and hatred every hour of every day. You are inescapably coming to the realization that your bitterness toward your offender is destroying you. You continue to drink the poison of bitterness in hopes it will kill your offender, but are compelled by undeniable realities that it is your own inward self being eaten up by the acidity of your unforgiving spirit. You only need to ingest the smallest amount of strychnine to produce severe effects.

As scandalous as it may appear to humanly conceived reasoning, what you need is the same kind of repentance from your sin and the same faith toward God by which He calls and commands your abuser. Extend to your abuser the offer of forgiveness. If he meets the conditions commanded by the gospel—repents, places faith in Christ, confesses, and seeks your pardon—then apply to your abuser the grace of forgiveness. Release your offender. In so doing, you will release yourself! In so doing, you will find peace and rest. In so doing, you will apply the gospel to your own case, and you will experience the healing balm your bruised body, battered mind, and broken heart so desperately need.

In cases where the abuser will not come to repentance and confession or when the abused cannot forgive and release their violator, the counselor will need to consider the following things: 1) Be exceedingly patient. The enormity of these kind of offenses often takes significant time to move the abused and abuser to a settled commitment to apply the ethic of the gospel. 2) Commit the need of the abused or abuser to ardent prayers. If Jesus taught that some cases of demonic possession can only be resolved by prayer, then cases of abuse so wickedly energized by

CONCLUSION

Satan demand nothing less than continued prayer. 3) When the abused struggle to grip the wisdom of the gospel in recognizing their own sin, extending the offer of forgiveness to a repentant abuser, and refuse to allow embedded bitterness to further poison them, the counselor must repeat, over and over, with all longsuffering and teaching, the genius of the gospel as outlined in this book. 4) Realize your duty is not to convince people of the correct biblical reaction to cases of sin. Your duty is to simply declare the genius of these gospel principles and to repeatedly knead them into the dough of the lives of those being counseled and commit the rest to God. When a victim of sin or violator of another person absolutely refuses to accept or follow the counsel of the gospel, the counselor must leave them to follow their own conscience without attempting to coerce them.

The 2018 book, *A Pilgrim's Guide to Rest*, fabulously expresses the relief of soul experienced by an individual who grips the wonder of forgiveness. The author cites the famous Christian allegory, *The Pilgrims Progress*. At the point where Christian stands at the cross of Christ and is finally freed from the terrible burden and guilt of his sin, Bunyan writes: "So I saw in my dream, that just as Christian came up with the cross, his burden loosed from off his shoulders, and fell from off his back, and began to tumble, and so continued to do, till it came to the mouth of the sepulcher, where it fell in, and I saw it no more."[7]

---

[7] John Bunyan, *The Pilgrim's Progress*, edited by Roger Pooley (New York: Penguin, 2008).

"It fell in, and I saw it no more." Bunyan profoundly captures the sensation of forgiveness: *weightlessness*. No doubt this is the most eloquent and doctrinal passages in all Christian fiction (apologies to Lewis fans). I have always appreciated the fact that Bunyan made the pilgrim stand there a while in bewilderment beneath the foolishness of the Cross. It would do the Church good to linger here a while longer than we typically do. Imputation, in all of its mystery, captivates the forgiven.[8]

My earnest and most fervent prayer for any person is that they will experience the removal of the weight of burden that sin places on the soul. When sin is removed from the guilty sinner by the all-glorious forgiveness found in the gospel of Christ, it becomes the prevailing inspiration for receiving forgiveness and for forgiving others. They have freely received forgiveness and they will freely give forgiveness. It is glorious indeed!

---

[8] Bryan Yawn, *A Pilgrims Guide to Rest* (Nashville, TN: Theocast, Inc., 2018), 97–98.

www.ingramcontent.com/pod-product-compliance
Lightning Source LLC
Chambersburg PA
CBHW070843160426
43192CB00012B/2290